ROOTS

BY **TARA O'CONNOR**

EDITOR-IN-CHIEF: CHRIS STAROS.

EDITED BY CHRIS STAROS & ZAC BOONE.

DESIGNED BY GILBERTO LAZCANO WITH CRYSSY CHEUNG.

PUBLISHED BY TOP SHELF PRODUCTIONS, PO BOX 1282, MARIETTA, GA 30061-1282, USA. TOP SHELF PRODUCTIONS IS AN IMPRINT OF IDW PUBLISHING, A DIVISION OF IDEA AND DESIGN WORKS, LLC. OFFICES: 2765 TRUXTUN ROAD, SAN DIEGO, CA 92106. TOP SHELF PRODUCTIONS®, THE TOP SHELF LOGO, IDEA AND DESIGN WORKS®, AND THE IDW LOGO ARE REGISTERED TRADEMARKS OF IDEA AND DESIGN WORKS, LLC. ALL RIGHTS RESERVED. WITH THE EXCEPTION OF SMALL EXCERPTS OF ARTWORK USED FOR REVIEW PURPOSES, NONE OF THE CONTENTS OF THIS PUBLICATION MAY BE REPRINTED WITHOUT THE PERMISSION OF IDW PUBLISHING. IDW PUBLISHING DOES NOT READ OR ACCEPT UNSOLICITED SUBMISSIONS OF IDEAS, STORIES, OR ARTWORK.

VISIT OUR ONLINE CATALOG AT WWW.TOPSHELFCOMIX.COM.

ISBN 978-1-60309-417-7

PRINTED IN KOREA.

17 18 19 20 21   5 4 3 2 1

O DIA GAC AON CABAIR

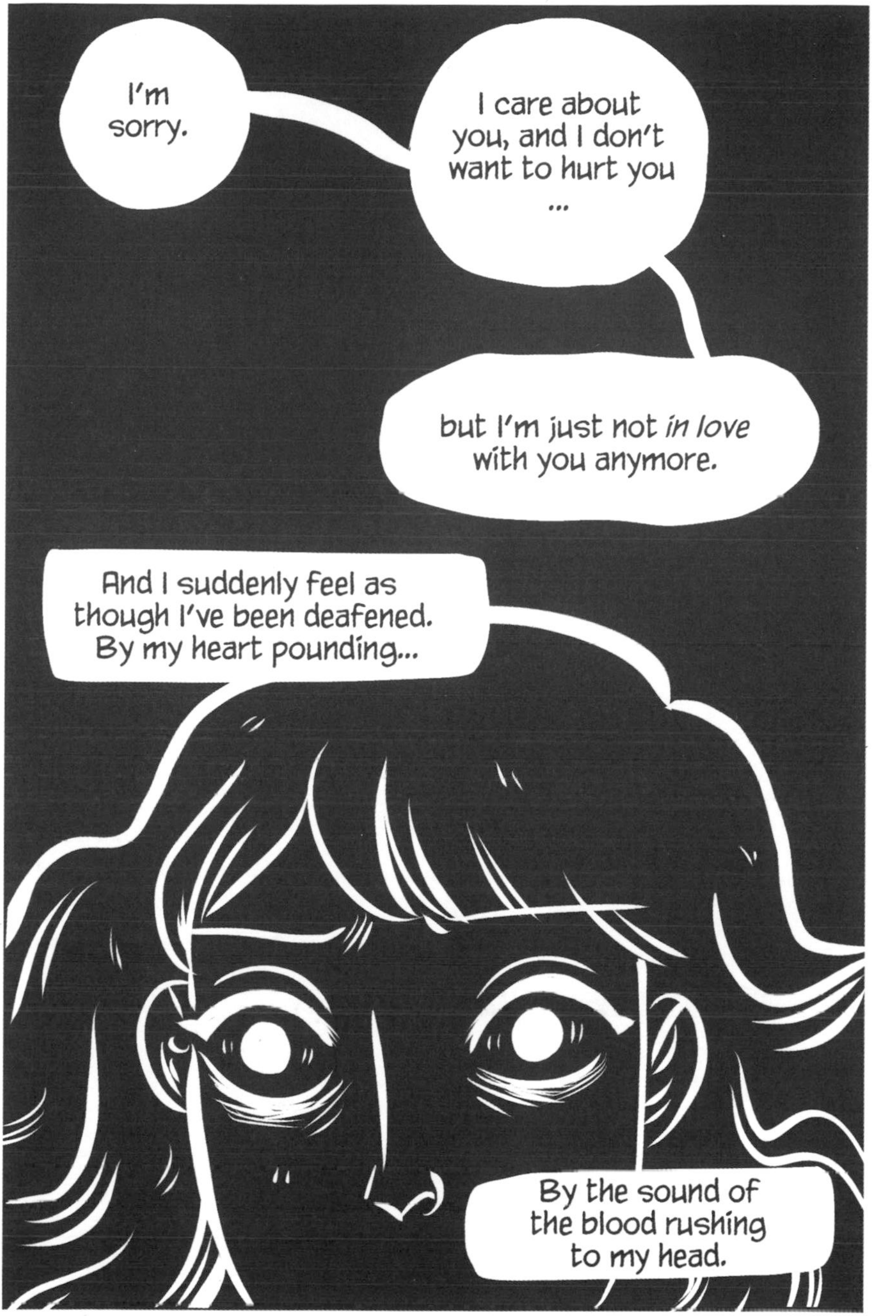
I'm sorry.
I care about you, and I don't want to hurt you ...
but I'm just not *in love* with you anymore.
And I suddenly feel as though I've been deafened. By my heart pounding...
By the sound of the blood rushing to my head.

Harsh as it is, deep down, I know...

I've known it for years, but never wanted to admit it.

It's all in your head!

You're over-thinking this!

I was wrong. It was really just

Denial

Denial that my world was changing. Denial that maybe I fell out of love too...

We were too scared to admit what was wrong, so we ignored our problems...

...and each other.

I was no help. My job barely gave me any hours from week to week.

When I wasn't working, I was drawing and writing comics.

Trying to make it!

With no hours came no money, so I was just barely able to buy food.

$12.62, please.

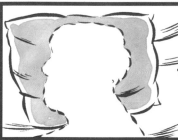

We were strangers sharing a bed.

7

Over time the thoughts became overwhelming.

Don't get up

I'll use all the heat

Use all the coffee

the electricity

I felt so guilty, so selfish. I knew he was fighting his own battles, but I couldn't help him. He wouldn't let me in.

For years I felt like I was just taking up space. That I was unwanted, that I was less than a person. I confided in only a few, and while talking helped, I still felt lost.

Alone.

We were friends
on the better days,
but it wasn't what either
of us wanted.

Or
deserved.

We tried,
but it wasn't
enough...

...there was too
much resentment
on both sides, and
I feared it would ruin
what friendship
remained.

We waited too long.

"True love will find you in the end, you'll find out
just who was your friend. Don't be sad, I know you will,
but don't give up until, true love will find you
in the end."
—Daniel Johnston

With heavy hearts...

...we realize...

...it's over.

Music is especially poignant...

And of course, by "home," I mean my childhood bedroom.

Ah! You're back again, I see.

Tara
Age: 16

Tara
Age: 19

Tara
Age: 23

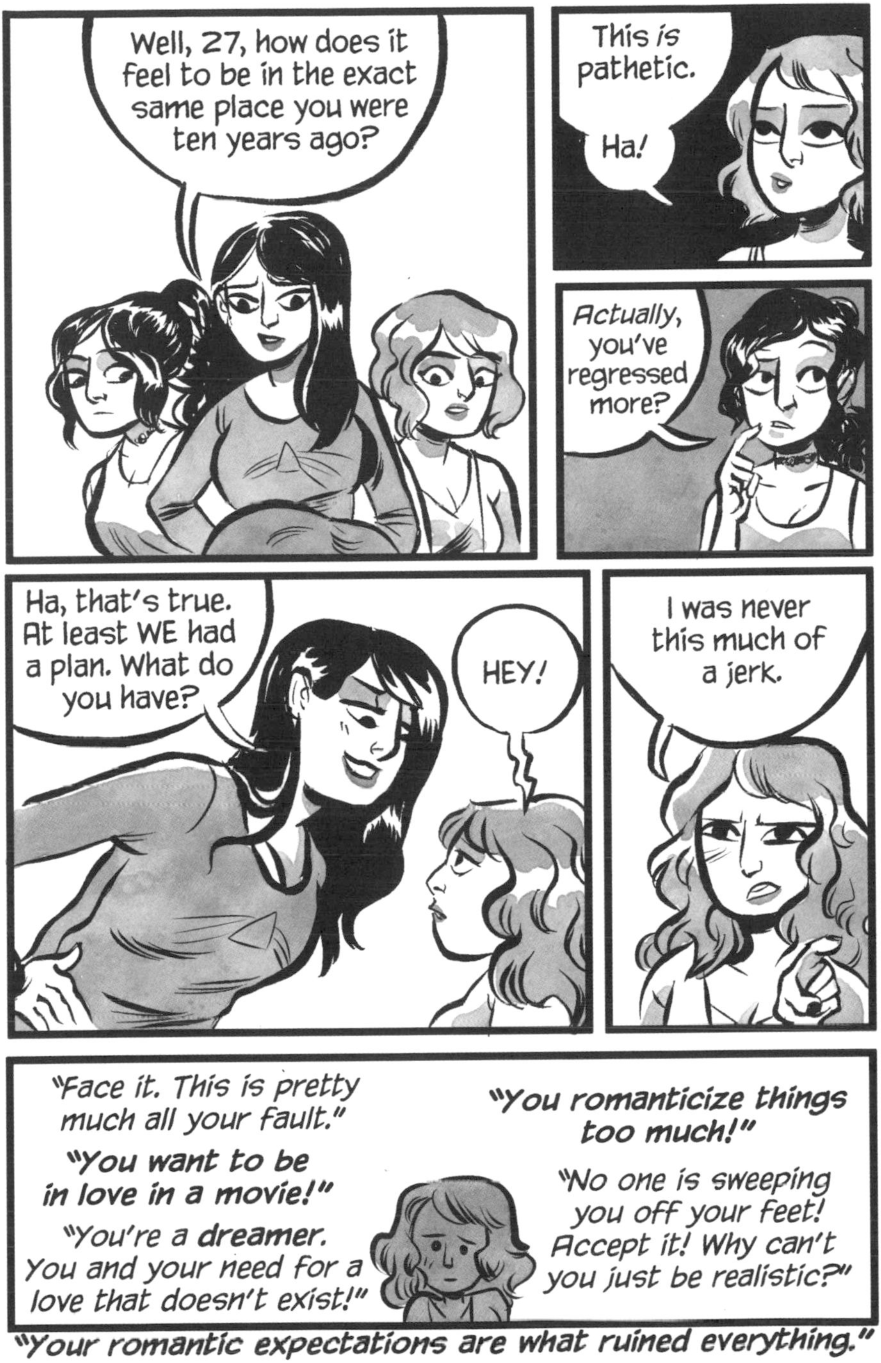
Well, 27, how does it feel to be in the exact same place you were ten years ago?
This *is* pathetic.
Ha!
Actually, you've regressed more?
Ha, that's true. At least WE had a plan. What do you have?
HEY!
I was never this much of a jerk.
"Face it. This is pretty much all your fault."
"You want to be in love in a movie!"
"You're a **dreamer.** You and your need for a love that doesn't exist!"
"You romanticize things too much!"
"No one is sweeping you off your feet! Accept it! Why can't you just be realistic?"
"Your romantic expectations are what ruined everything."

No, no. Well. That wasn't the only reason.

It didn't help though.

Seriously, what gives you any right to romanticize? Come on, now.

She's got a point, you know...

I mean, look at you!

Frizzy hair...

Pimples? Still? Pasty skin ...

Not to mention, you're clingy as hell.

Who wants that?

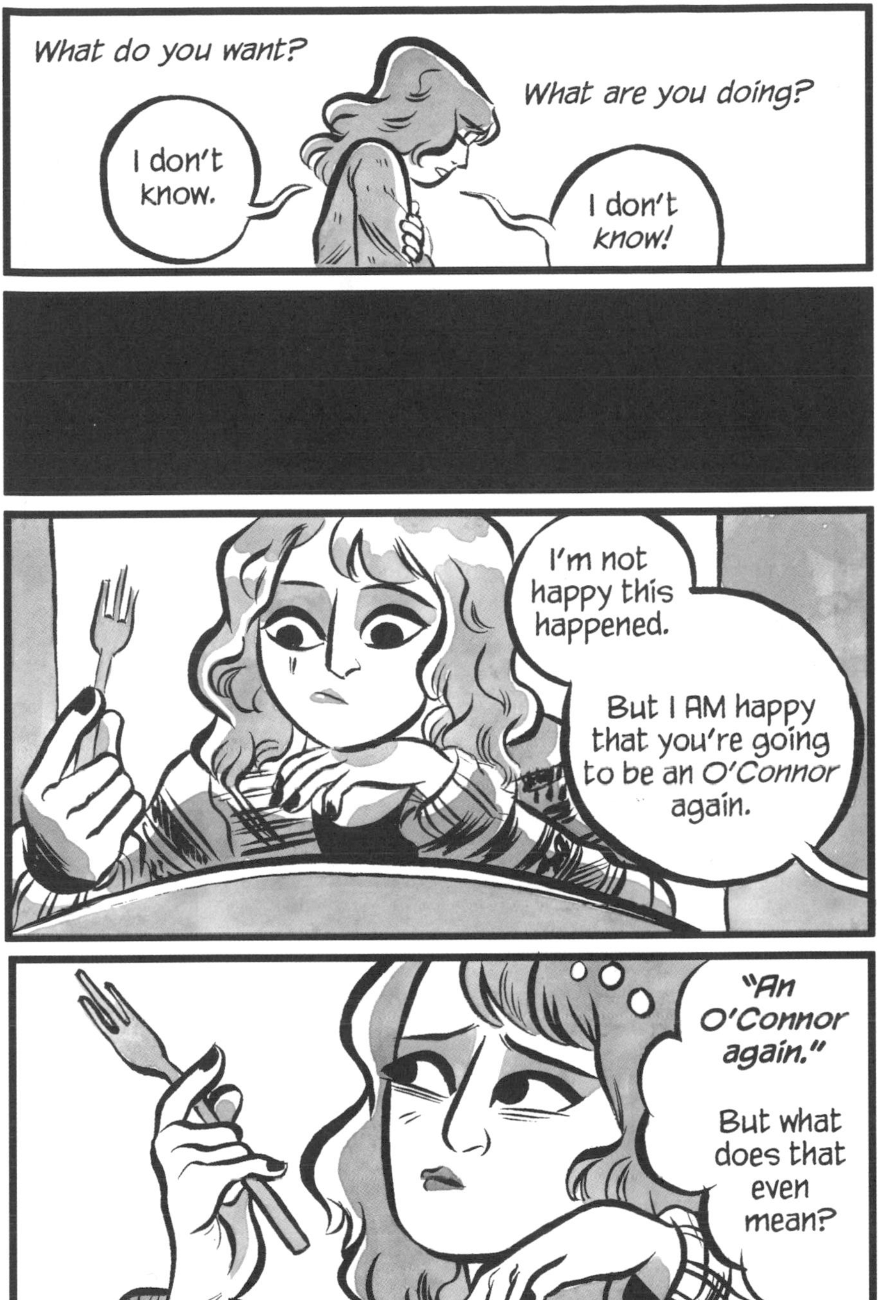
What do you want?
I don't know.
What are you doing?
I don't know!
I'm not happy this happened.
But I AM happy that you're going to be an O'Connor again.
"An O'Connor again."
But what does that even mean?

And once again, music lends a hand.

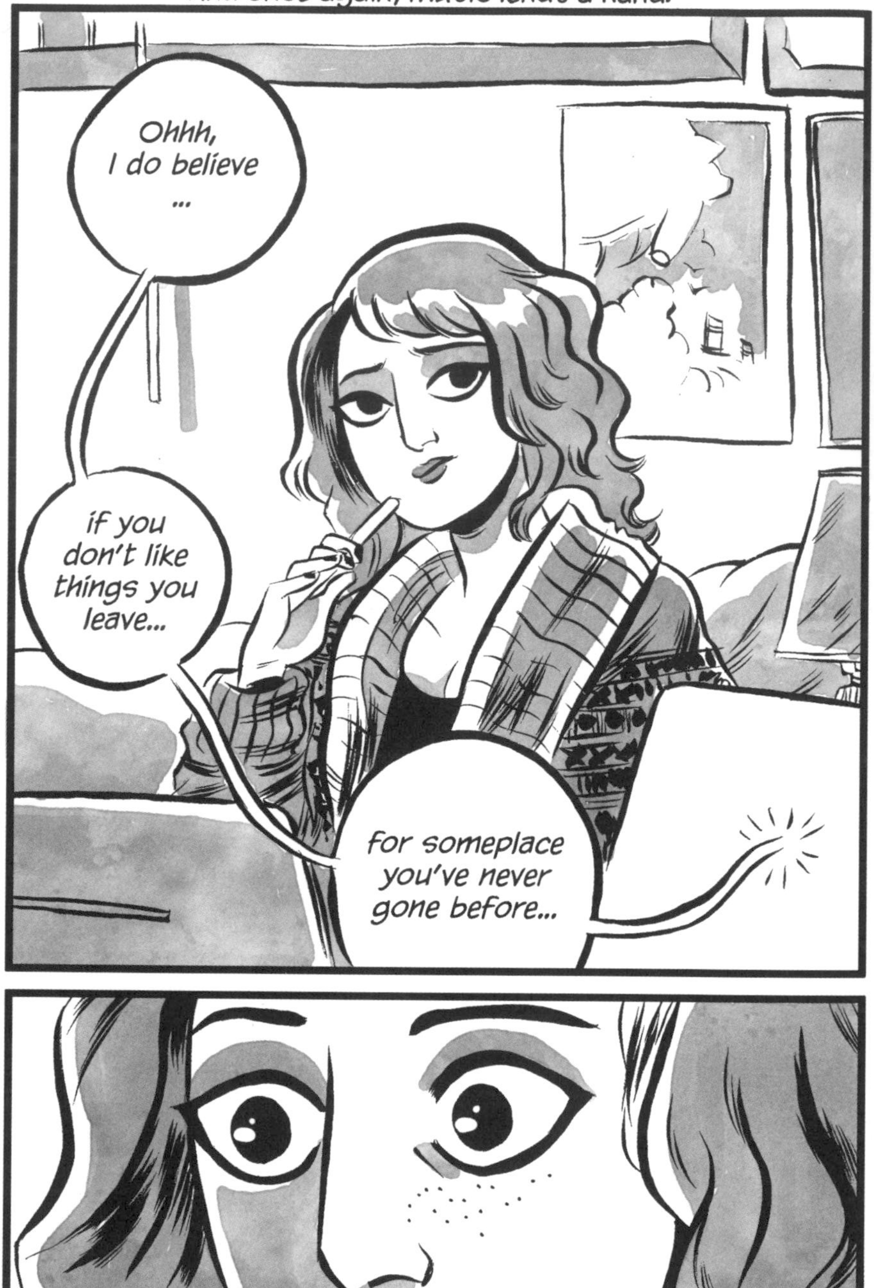
Ohhh, I do believe ...
if you don't like things you leave...
for someplace you've never gone before...

Ooh, I do believe you are what you perceive ...

what comes is better than what came before.

And, little by little, the idea for *Roots* comes to light.

I've always been interested in my family history, but beyond my parents, I was never told much about it.

O DIA GAC AON CABAIR

Of course, there were the O'Connors,
and the Coyles from my mother's side, but
who else? The Wards? The Templemans?

I talk a bit with my family, immediate
and extended, and I get a few tremendously
wonderful leads. My brain feels like it's over-
flowing with ideas, and one thing pops
into my head: travelogue.

What if I make a comic about this, all of this?
The break-up, my heritage, my journey of
finding myself again? Could I?

Once I have a good jumping-off point, I can really start planning out the book. Comics have always been an outlet for me, and what better way to process my world being flipped on its head?

...me here!

...nyway that I possibly ...there, it'll be great!

Ahhhhhhhhh you're great enough, I h works out

OK

Start a proj

And after many days and many, many conversations, I realize that I CAN do this. It's something I've always wanted to do, and I feel like I finally have that chance. I'm scared, and excited, and nervous. Will this click of a mouse change my life?*

*Yes.

The next few months are filled with great things!

Launching *Roots* as a crowd-funded comic!

Hey there, Kickstarter!

Finally getting my passport!

D-do you want a brush or something?

Ah, my hair always looks like this.

But... thanks?

ROOTS GETTING FUNDED! WOO!

gratulations!

project was successfully fu

Roots: A C

$5,316.00
USD
pledged

ROOTS
IRELAND

Funded!

AAAAH

But they're also filled with not-so-great things.

Never being able to get any sleep.

Picking up the last of my stuff.

Going to sign divorce papers.

Um...

is someone here?

Tara? Here you go.

He overnighted them to us yesterday, isn't that great?

Um.

OK?

And just like that, it was done.

I didn't even get to sit down.

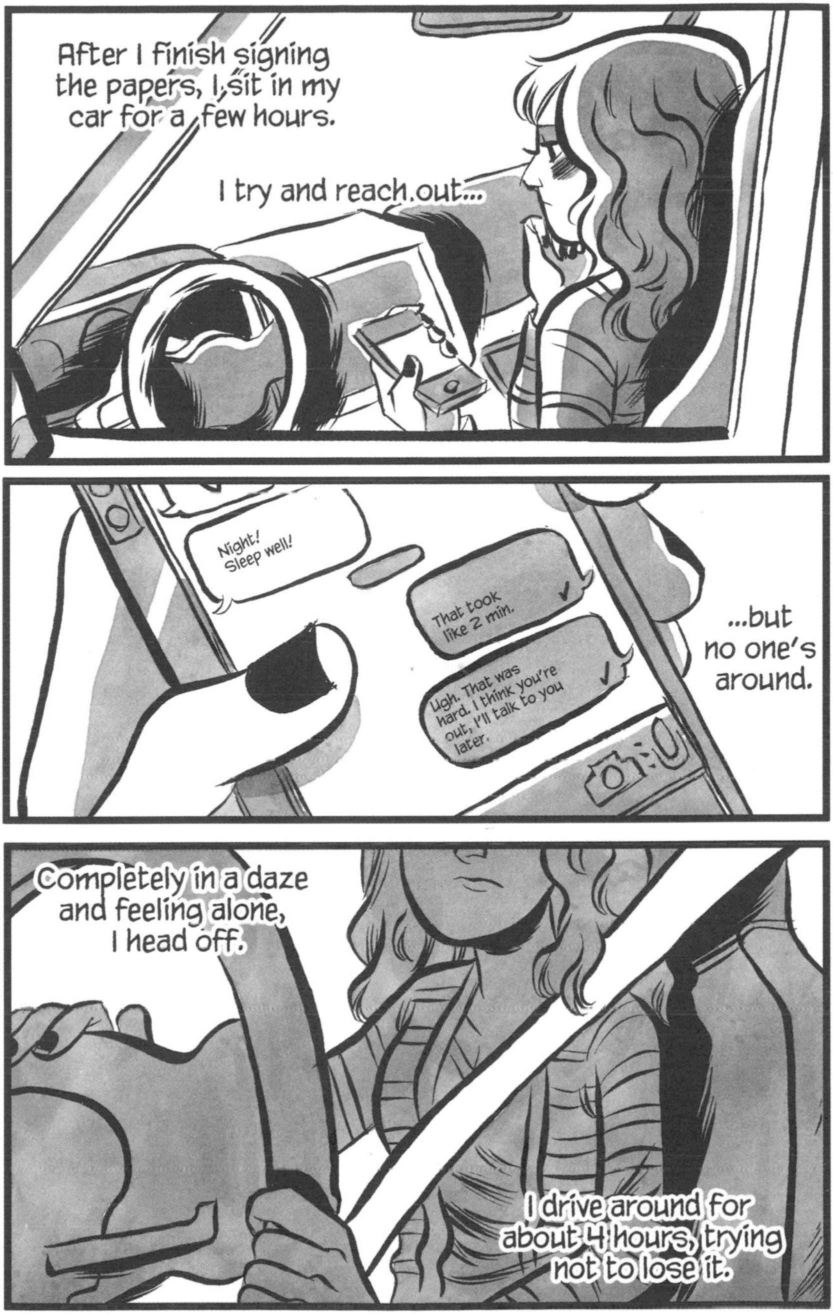
After I finish signing the papers, I sit in my car for a few hours.
I try and reach out...
Night! Sleep well!
That took like 2 min.
Ugh. That was hard. I think you're out, I'll talk to you later.
...but no one's around.
Completely in a daze and feeling alone, I head off.
I drive around for about 4 hours, trying not to lose it.

Arrive back at the house to find that it's empty.

So naturally I handle it in the worst ways imaginable!

Complain and whine endlessly on twitter.

Tara O'Connor @TaraOComics 30m

UGHH this suck

Tara O'Connor @TaraOComics 33m

Worst day ever n

Tara O'Connor @TaraOComics 39m

Finally home this

Drink copious amounts of wine.

Angrily drunk text people.

Knowing there is no sleep in sight, I put in a comfort flick and tune everything else out.

Hey, it's a kind of magic.*

*Highlander

The night drags on, and I'm left alone with my thoughts.

If it's the right thing to do, why are you so upset about all of this?

I come to realize that I'm in mourning.

My life is going to be completely different from what I imagined only a few months ago.

I'm mourning the future I thought I was going to have.

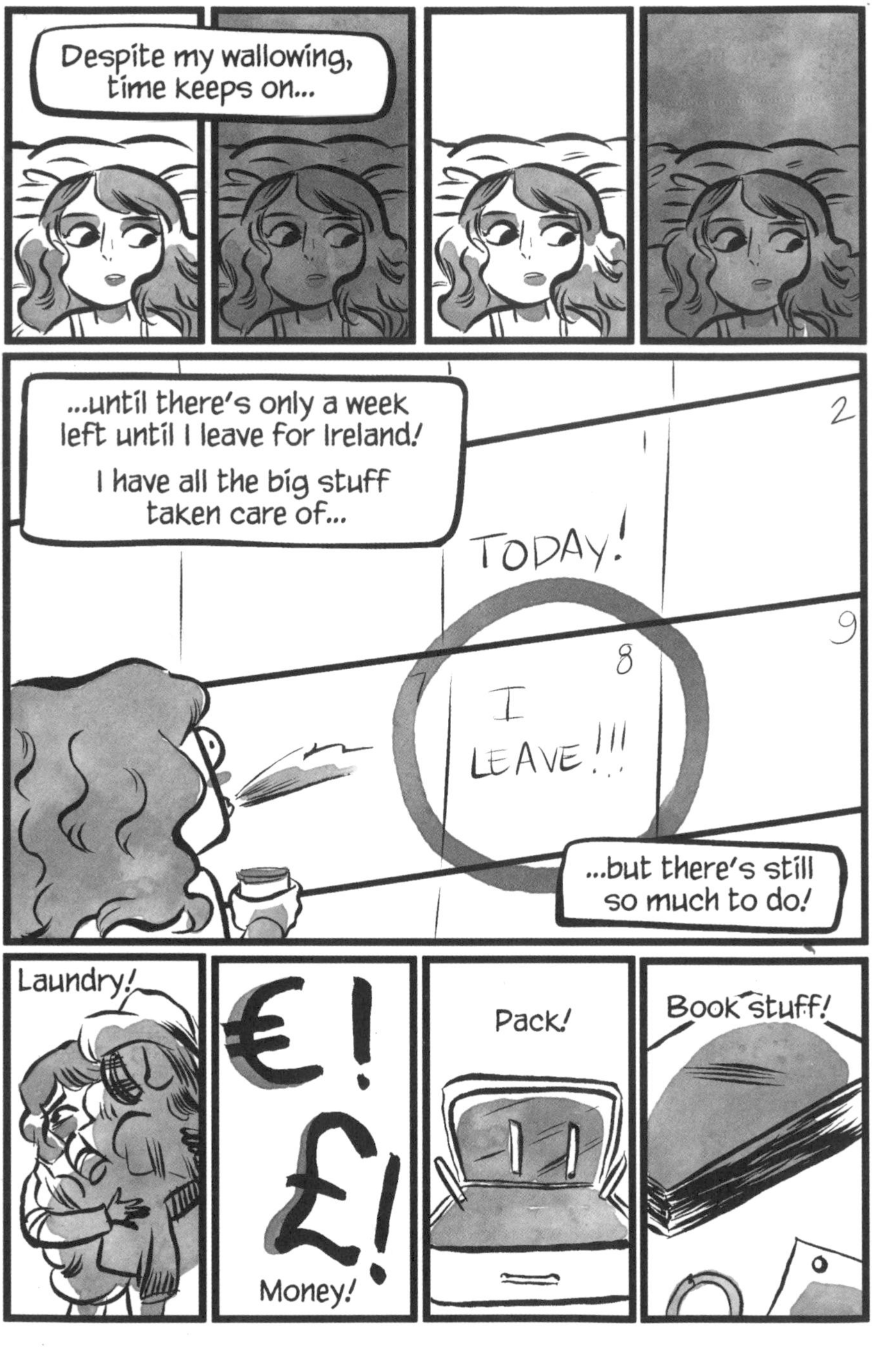
Despite my wallowing, time keeps on...
...until there's only a week left until I leave for Ireland!
I have all the big stuff taken care of...
2
TODAY!
9
8
7
I LEAVE!!!
...but there's still so much to do!
Laundry!
€!
£!
Money!
Pack!
Book stuff!

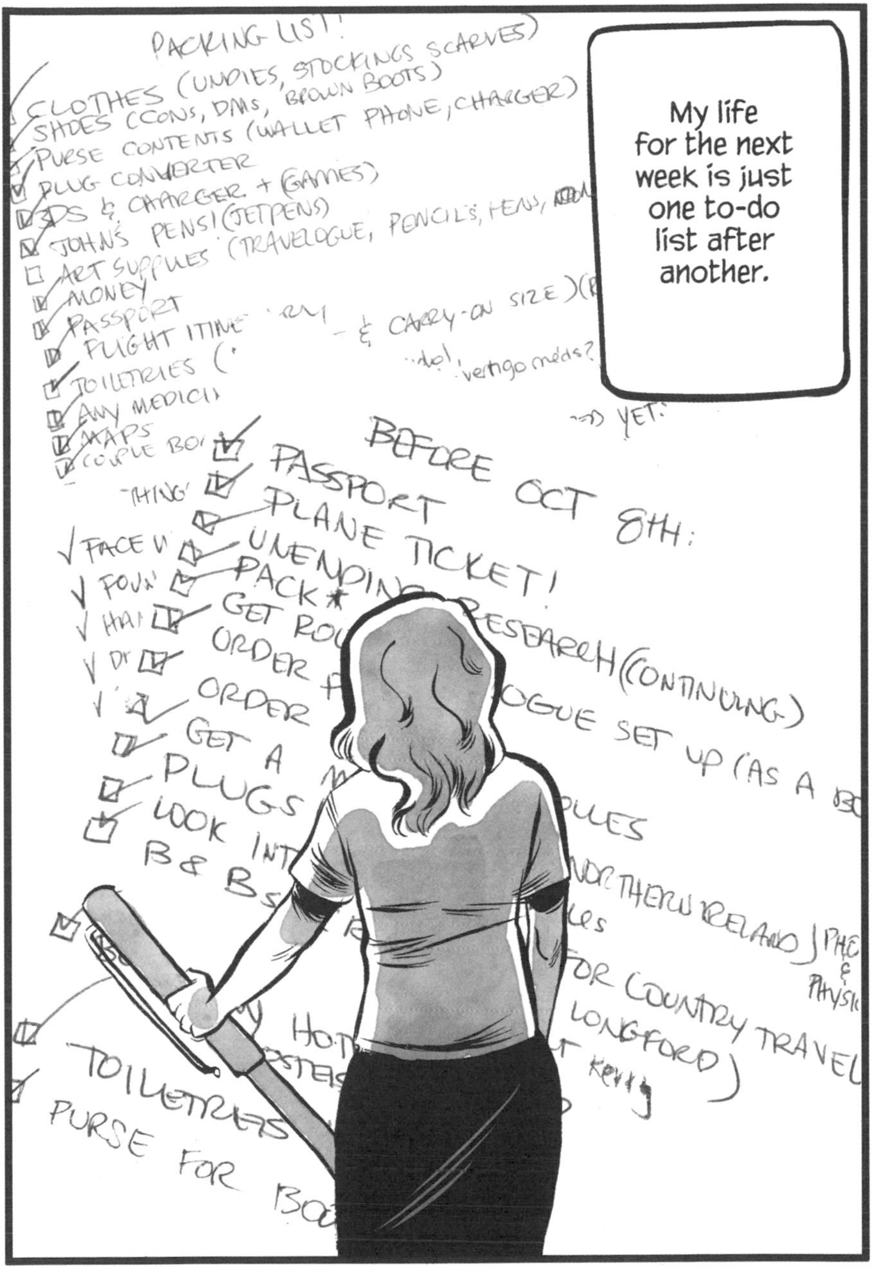

My life for the next week is just one to-do list after another.
PACKING LIST!
CLOTHES (UNDIES, STOCKINGS SCARVES)
SHOES (CONS, DMS, BROWN BOOTS)
PURSE CONTENTS (WALLET PHONE, CHARGER)
PLUG CONVERTER
3DS & CHARGER + GAMES)
JOHN'S PENS! (JETPENS)
ART SUPPLIES (TRAVELOGUE, PENCILS, PENS,
MONEY
PASSPORT
CARRY-ON SIZE)
vertigo meds?
BEFORE OCT 8TH:
PASSPORT
PLANE TICKET!
PACK
RESEARCH (CONTINUING)
ORDER
SET UP (AS A
GET A
PLUGS
LOOK
B & B
NORTHERN IRELAND
FOR COUNTRY TRAVEL
LONGFORD)
TOILETRIES
PURSE FOR

And then... it's finally time!

Before too long, I find myself at security. Despite never having been out of the States before, I'm surprisingly at ease. I am a little nervous, but it all feels very natural. I take that as the very best of signs.

So I say my farewells...

See you in a month!

...go through security...

(or a magical girl power-up?)

CNN

EBOL

...and find my way to gate 95.

...TO DUBLIN, PLEASE PROCEED TO GATE 82... I REPEAT...

There's a gate change, but soon we're back on track...

...and ready to board.

I get to talking to a few nice folks while waiting in line.

BOARDING GROUP 3

So, are you heading home then?

Huh?

Oh! No, no, I'm just visiting.

I wish!

Why do I want to say YES?

Here we go!

Find my seat.

Pillows?

AND

Blankets?

LUXURYYYY!

Thanks for flying the friendly skies.

Ha!

uhh...

very...

Our pilots are...

um. Professional?

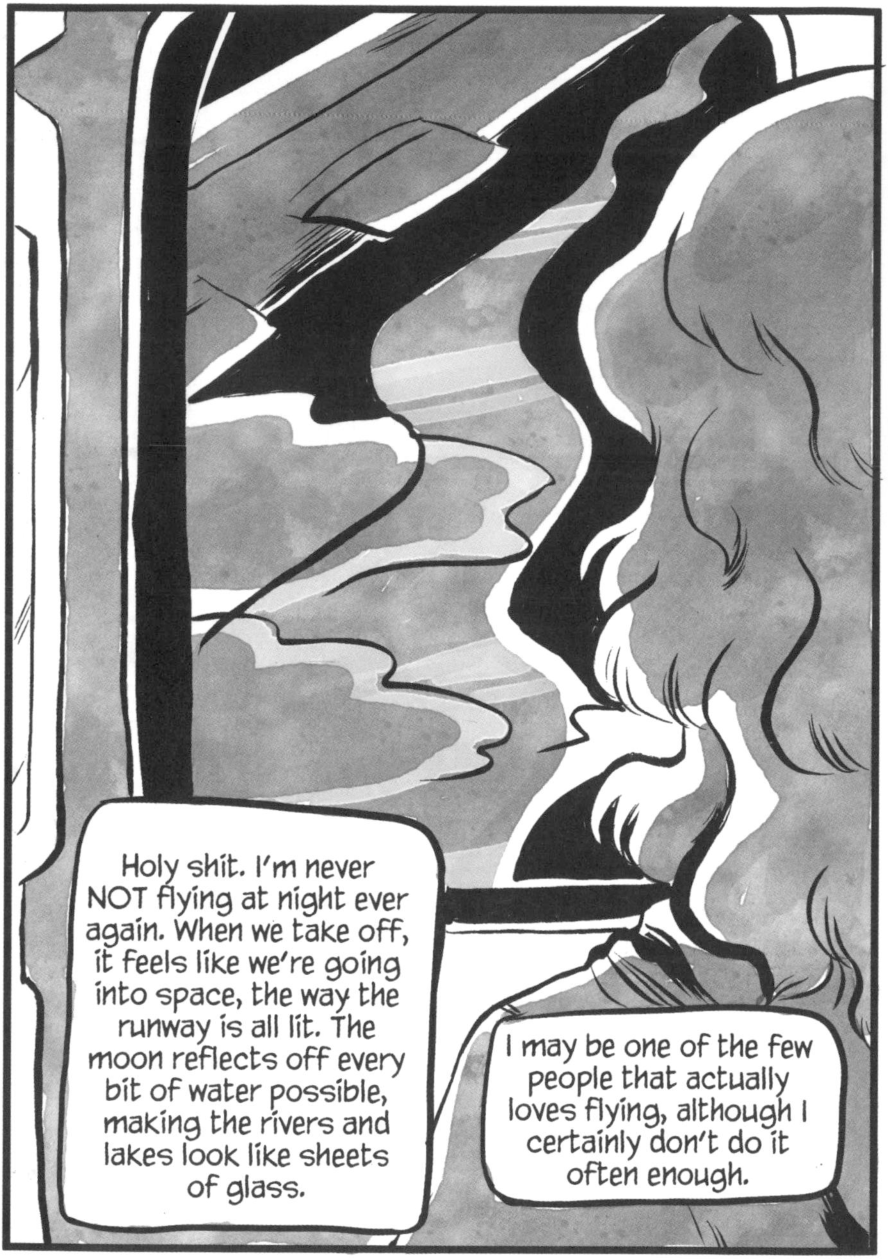
Holy shit. I'm never NOT flying at night ever again. When we take off, it feels like we're going into space, the way the runway is all lit. The moon reflects off every bit of water possible, making the rivers and lakes look like sheets of glass.
I may be one of the few people that actually loves flying, although I certainly don't do it often enough.

I spend the majority of the flight taking notes and looking out my window.

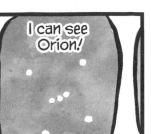

I can see Orion!

I make an effort to sleep, though I know it isn't going to happen.

I pass the time watching the travel screen, as well as repeats of *The Walking Dead.*

Much to the dismay of my seat mate.

Having never flown long enough to have a meal, this is my first experience with airline food!
(It wasn't THAT bad, but I was too excited to actually eat!)

10pm

Steamed chicken with noodles and lettuce.

4am

A croissant and some hard fruit.

I slowly start to notice small lights and realize that we're once again over land!

Ladies and gentlemen...

we'll be starting our descent into Dublin shortly.

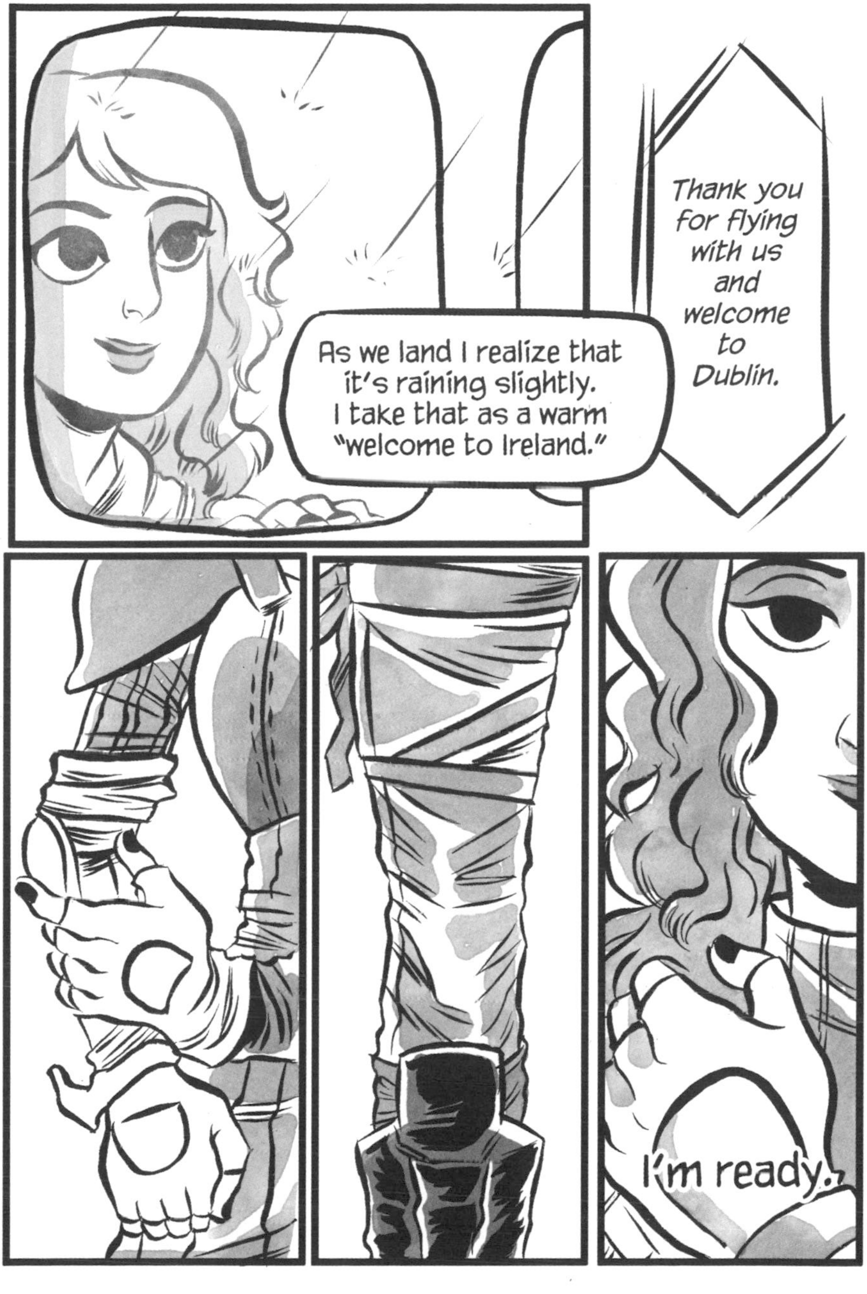
As we land I realize that it's raining slightly. I take that as a warm "welcome to Ireland."
Thank you for flying with us and welcome to Dublin.
I'm ready.

And now, your journey begins.

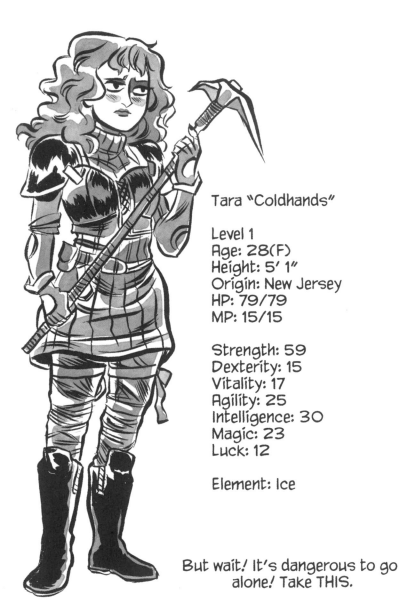

Tara "Coldhands"

Level 1
Age: 28(F)
Height: 5' 1"
Origin: New Jersey
HP: 79/79
MP: 15/15

Strength: 59
Dexterity: 15
Vitality: 17
Agility: 25
Intelligence: 30
Magic: 23
Luck: 12

Element: Ice

But wait! It's dangerous to go
alone! Take THIS.

It's John! I met him on twitter almost three years ago. Being of Ireland, he graciously offered his time to help me out with *Roots*!

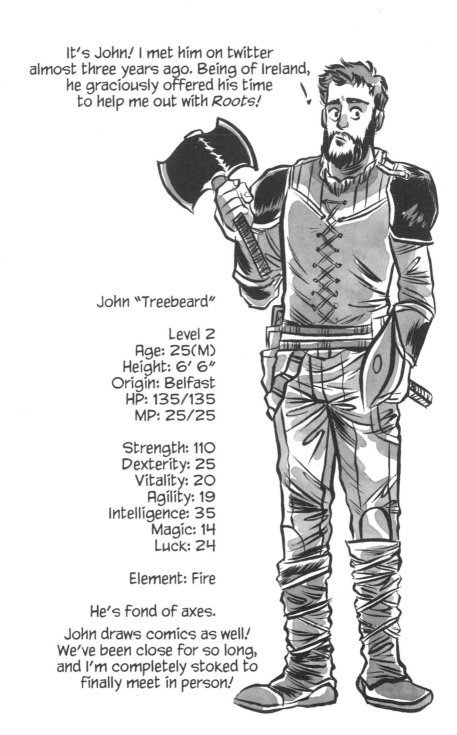

John "Treebeard"

Level 2
Age: 25(M)
Height: 6' 6"
Origin: Belfast
HP: 135/135
MP: 25/25

Strength: 110
Dexterity: 25
Vitality: 20
Agility: 19
Intelligence: 35
Magic: 14
Luck: 24

Element: Fire

He's fond of axes.

John draws comics as well! We've been close for so long, and I'm completely stoked to finally meet in person!

Once I pick up my bags and go through customs, I head out.

I spot him straightaway. I'm finally nervous. That's normal though, right?

Hey there, you.

We hug, and it suddenly feels as though there was never any distance between us.

We have some tea and a small chat about both of our trips. (He took a bus down from Belfast.)

Big surprise, we're both exhausted.

We're staying in town for a couple days.

Hoping, we have picked the right bus to the hotel, we sit and wait. The sun finally rises, and it stops raining.

I look out the window a lot while on the bus.

I may be in a different country, but it doesn't *feel* like I am.

Aside from the whole "driving on the other side of the road" bit.

FUUUUU—

BEWLEY'S

So we did wind up getting the wrong bus.

Haa. Sorry.

Hehe.

Awh, you're fine.

The driver kindly takes us as close as he can.

And with the help of GPS:

WHOA!

That's the hotel? It's massive!

Though we are insanely early for check-in:

Agggghh!

Finally. We made it!

We really shouldn't ...

I know, but I *reeeally* want to.

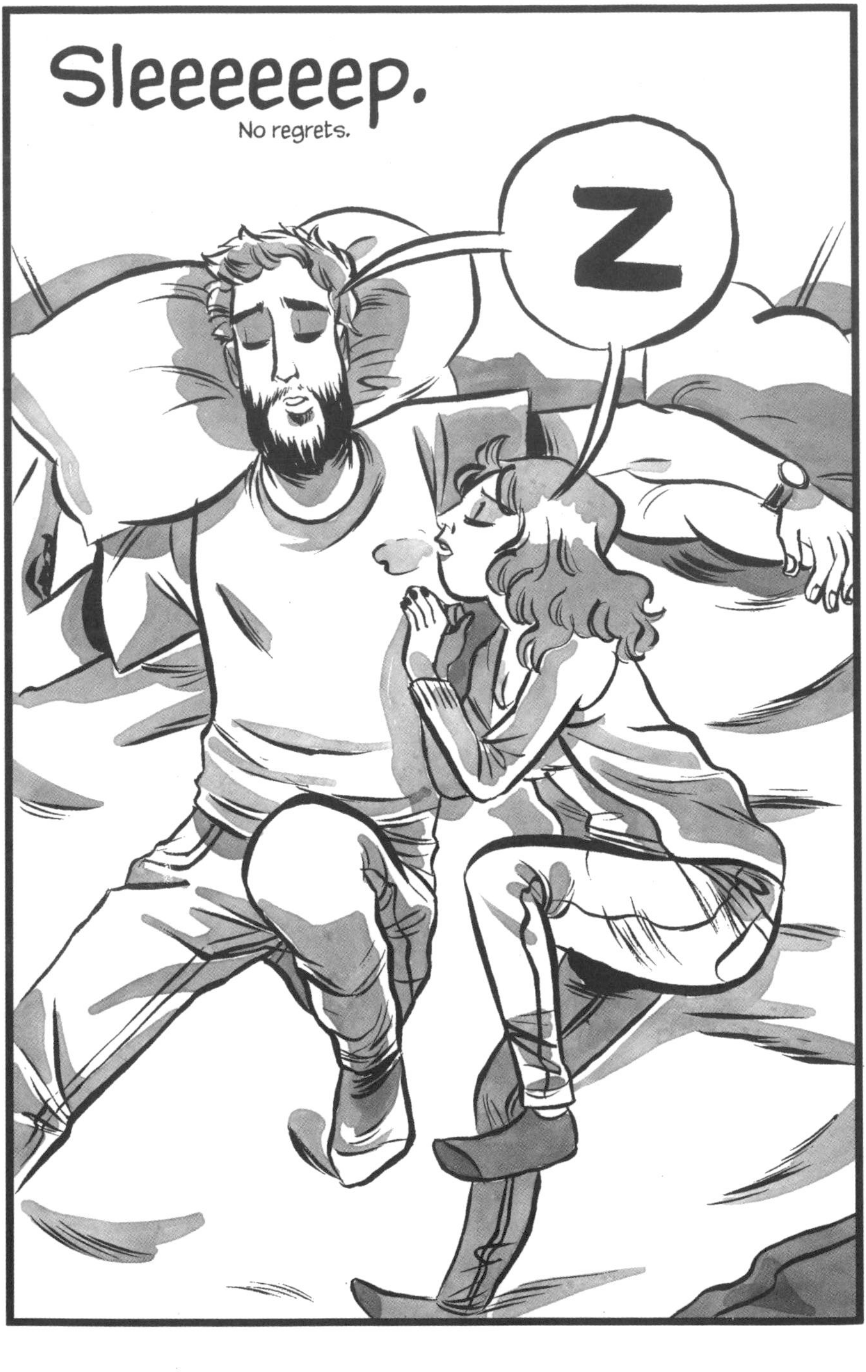
Sleeeeeeep.
No regrets.
Z

When we wake up, it's dark. Whoops.

We head out to explore Dublin at night.

PINTS!

Many pints.

I don't have a car yet, but it's fairly easy to get around by walking, and the weather is excellent.

Granted, we're technically outside of Dublin so it's relatively quiet, but it's a great little area.

We chill near a bridge and watch the water before heading back.

Aaaand there's the jet lag...

Take two aspirin...

...and head over to the window. I watch the streets; there are a few folks out still.

Otherwise, it's all quiet. Peaceful.

Unlike my head.

Can't sleep either?

So we feed our insomnia with:

You just shook your head ... doesn't that make you happy?*

and some tunes.

...I like chicken—

Pie.**

*The Princess Bride

** Crow Black Chicken- Ry Cooder

Great start.

Tara, being known by most for getting ill, gets ill. Shocker.

John sends me to bed and ventures to the downstairs of the hotel for some lunch.

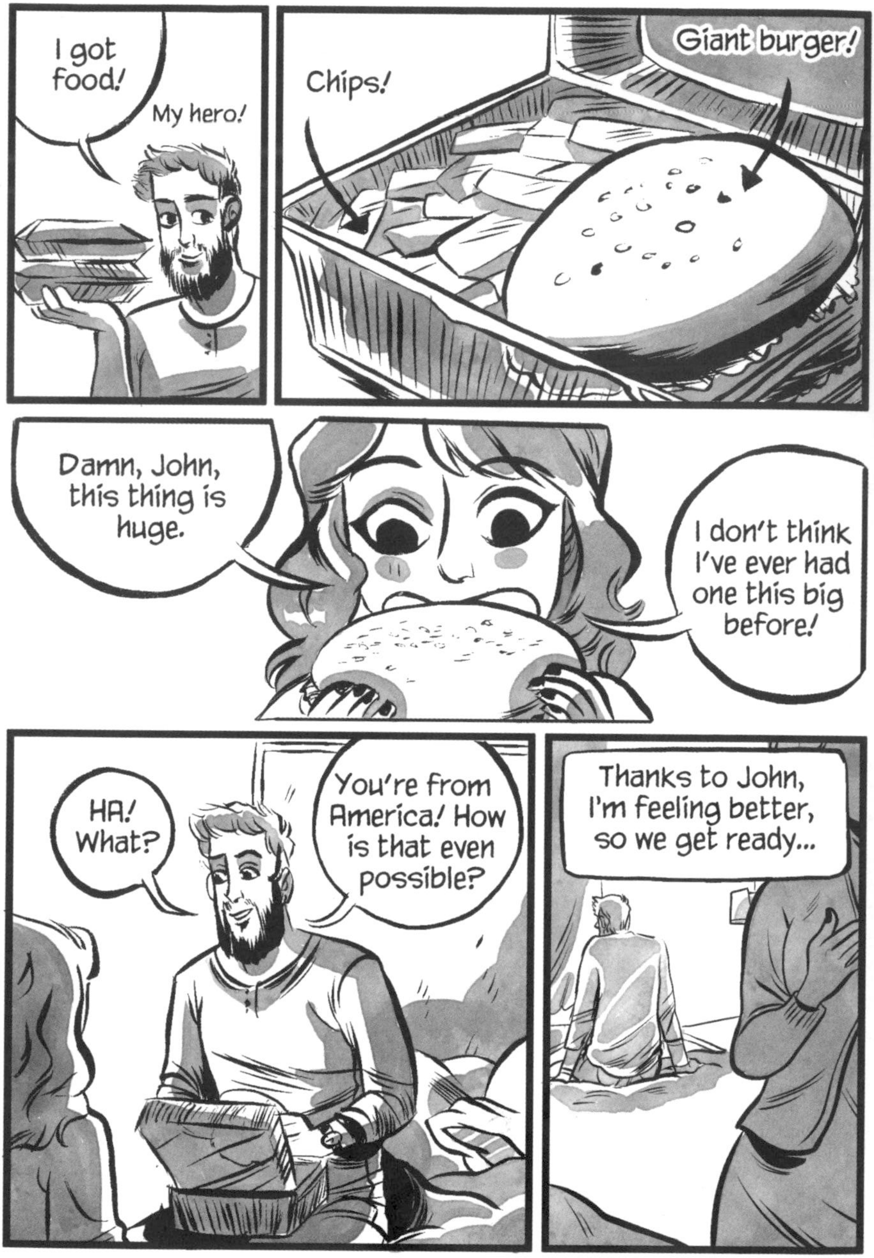
I got food!
My hero!
Chips!
Giant burger!
Damn, John, this thing is huge.
I don't think I've ever had one this big before!
HA! What?
You're from America! How is that even possible?
Thanks to John, I'm feeling better, so we get ready...

We set off and continue to explore the town.

We find a bar that seems fairly busy...

HA HA HA

And I was like, "NO WAY, MAN!"

I try my best to avoid obnoxious Americans.

(It doesn't work!)

Oh god, John, I can't escape them.

Some drinkies. Blue Moon and a Cabernet Sauvignon.

We pick the most deserted area we can find...

...and plan out the next few days, drowning out the lousy bar soundtrack.

47

Now, a little bit about the O'Connors.

My great-great-grandfather, Patrick, was supposedly born in Dublin on the 17th of March, 1848.

It seemed suspect to many of the family because of the date...

"Supposedly," 'cos we can't find his birth certificate.

...being born on St. Patrick's and being called Patrick...

...but it's probably more common than you'd think.

Patrick moved to England in 1873, and shortly after married a woman by the name of Mary.

Mary was born in Glasgow. Coincidentally, she was also born an O'Connor, but her parents, of Galway, moved to Scotland during the Great Famine. When they got there they dropped the "O" and went by "Connor."

Glasgow

Due to a lack of birth certificates, not much is known about Patrick's folks...

...but Mary's folks were Sarah McDade and Peter Connor.*

*So yes, my great-great-great-grandmother was Sarah Connor XD

49

Mary moved to Liverpool in 1871, where she worked as a housemaid.

Patrick, according to the census reports, worked as a seaman.

They met, and married, soon after.

In 1893, Mary passed away...

...and Patrick left for America with the rest of their family. Once there, he found work in the navy yard.

He resided in Brooklyn along with his children. Among them was Edward O'Connor, who would later meet and marry a Delia Ward.

Our last morning in Dublin, and it's time to go NORTH, but first—

Breakfast!

A fry, or a full breakfast consisting of bacon, sausage, bread, eggs, etc.

And a teeny tiny pot for tea!!

Once stuffed, we head back to the room to pack up.

I make sure I have my fare handy...

...and we wait for the bus.

EEEEEEEE

We catch a noisy bus to the airport where we'll catch one up to Belfast.

Again, I'm mesmerized by the landscape.

Strangely enough, the terrain isn't *that* much different from parts of northern New Jersey.

The second bus is much more quiet, thankfully, despite being packed.

I receive some reassuring glances from across the aisle.

Next stop: BELFAST.

John's dad picks us up at the bus depot, and we head back to his house.

And there I meet the family! They are the best for letting me share their home for a couple weeks.

Over tea I do my best to explain my plans for the trip and what I know so far about my roots.

My mind really is put at ease being here. It's been a long time since I've felt so content.

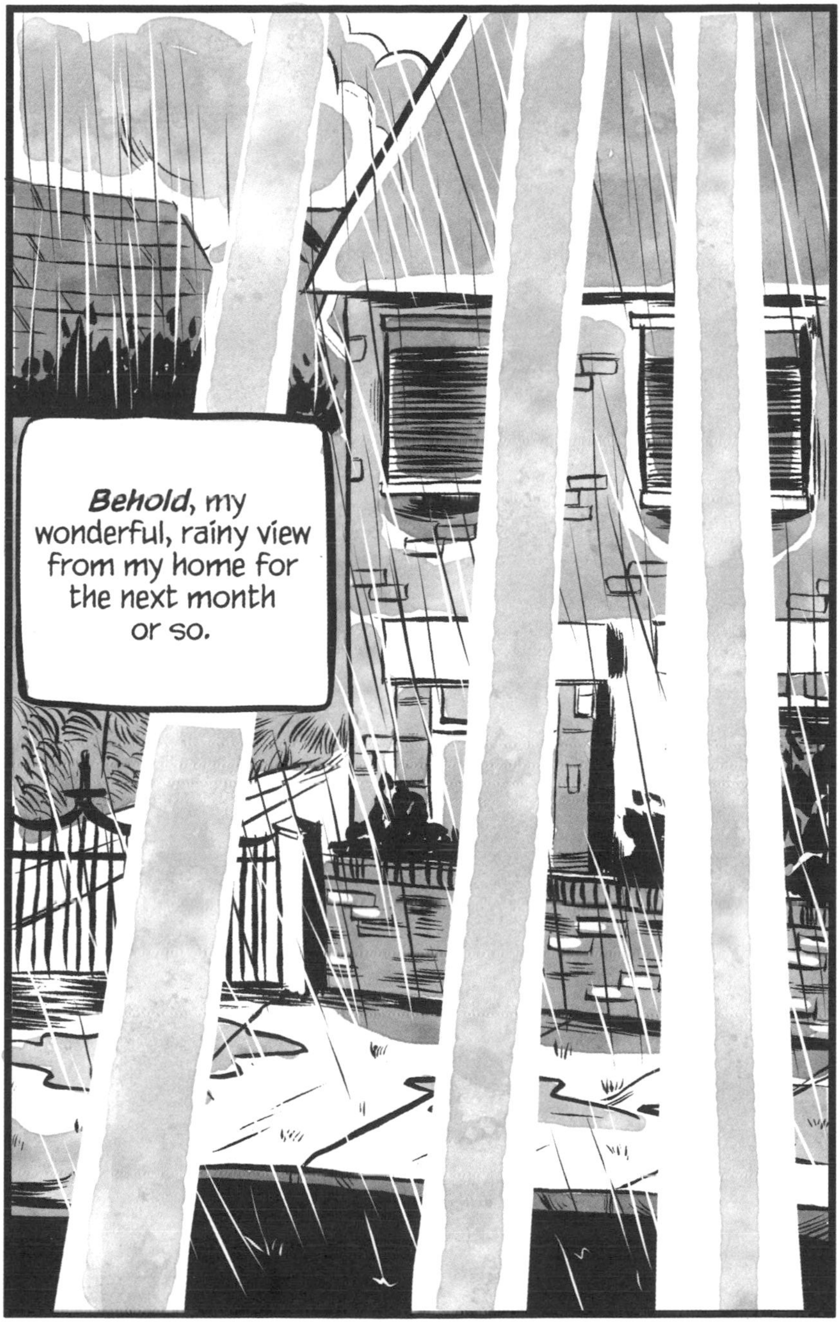
Behold, my wonderful, rainy view from my home for the next month or so.

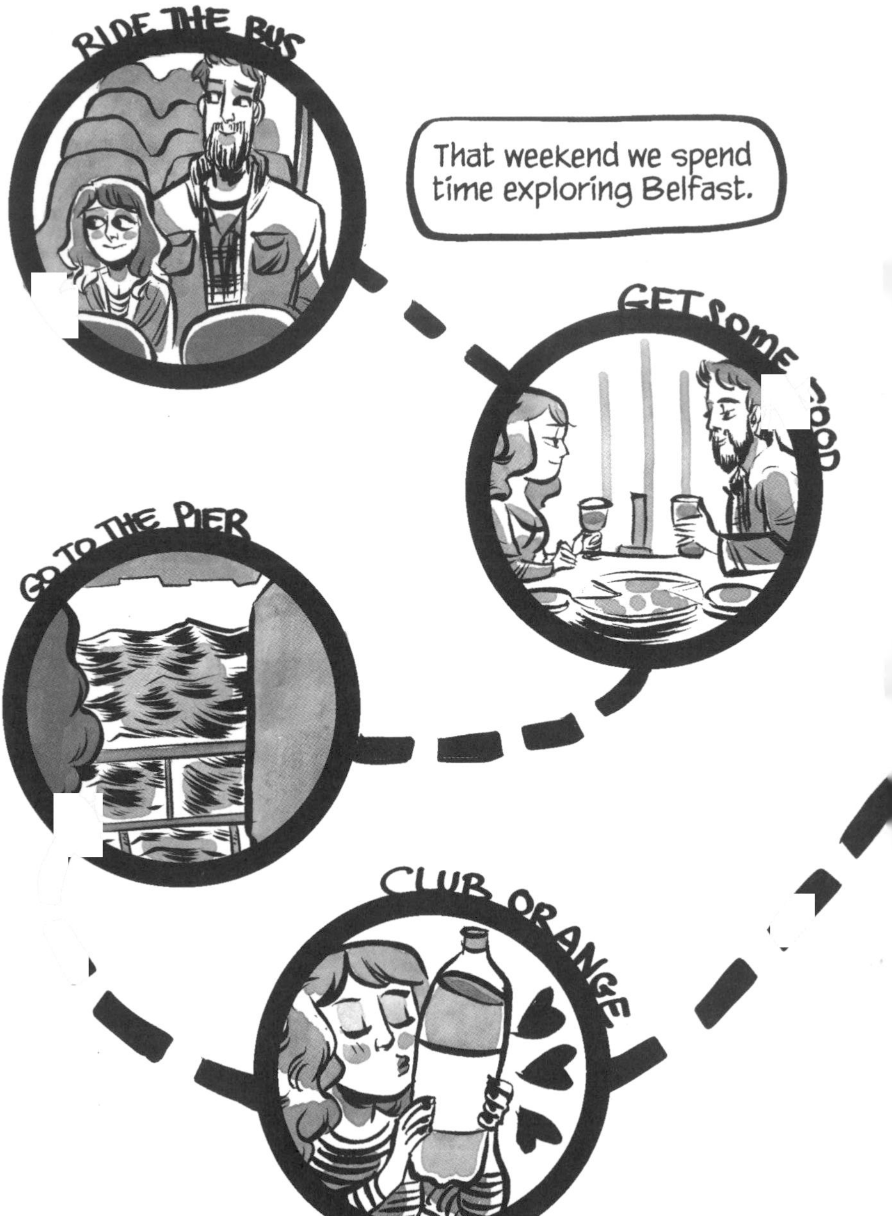
RIDE THE BUS
That weekend we spend time exploring Belfast.
GET SOME
GO TO THE PIER
CLUB ORANGE

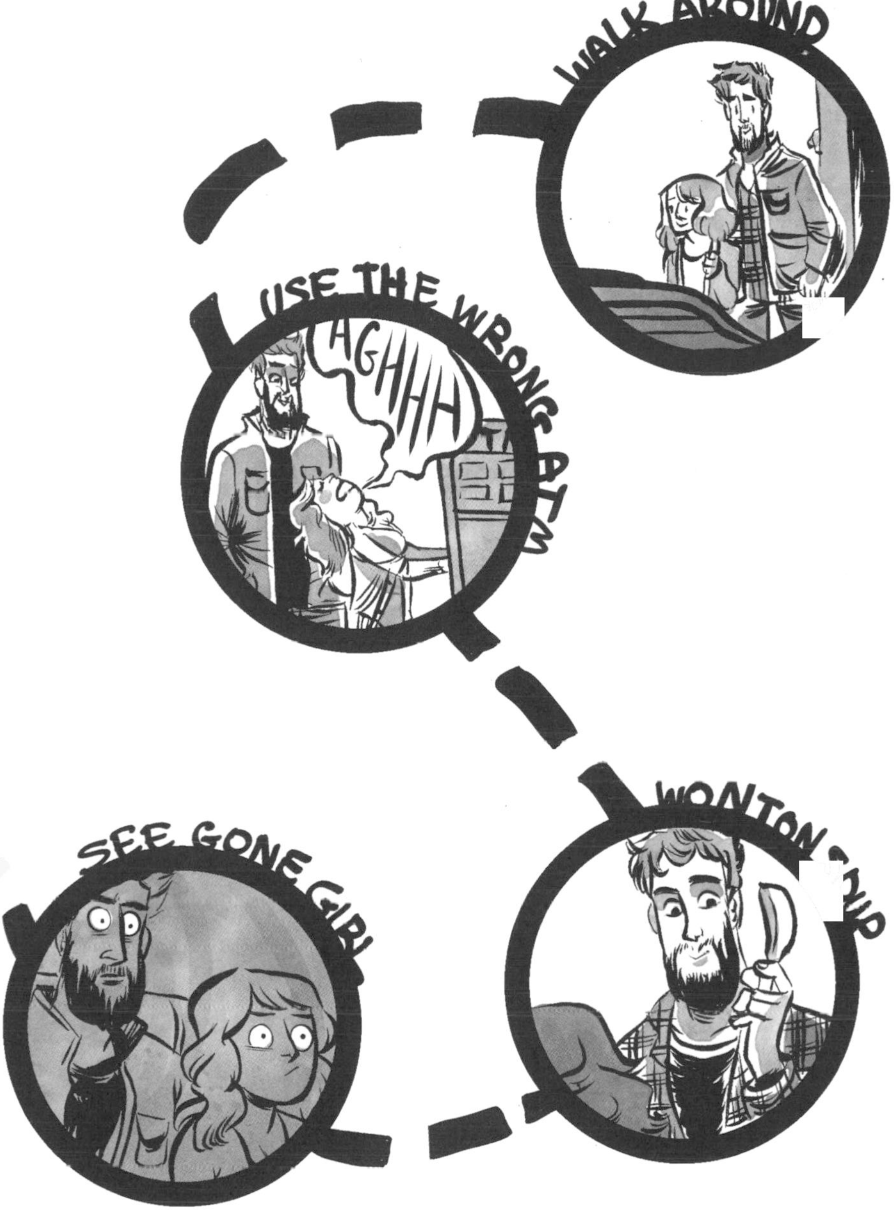
WALK AROUND
USE THE WRONG ATM
AGHHH
WONTON
SEE GONE GIRL

Over the course of the trip I became very acquainted with taking the bus.

These aren't even HALF of the receipts that I held onto.

It takes a bit before I actually know where we're going. I can usually follow John's lead and tell the driver "likewise" or "the same, please."

I tell John that buses where I live are few and far between. The nearest bus stop is 30 minutes by car!

I'm told that if you can't go down the stairs as the bus is moving, you'll be outed as a tourist.

I get it right the second time.
(Not that my accent isn't already a dead giveaway.)

Rental car time!

We've only the one.

Automatics are hard to come by, as it happens, BUT...

...we're soon on our way!

Luckily, I come from a state that still has roundabouts ...

Thanks, NJ!

Having prior experience with them helps tremendously!

After a couple of hours driving around, I feel comfortable.

I only hit the curb 4 times!

Sorry, John!

The next morning, we're off to Mohill, near where some of my ancestors lived.

With John as my navigator, we head down south.

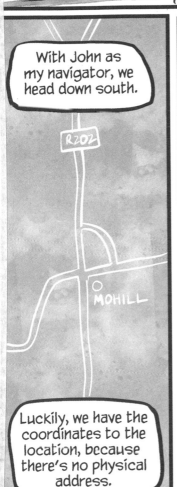

R202

MOHILL

Luckily, we have the coordinates to the location, because there's no physical address.

And then we take a right up ahead.

The area is just gorgeous.

Narrow country roads surrounded by farmland and trees.

It feels like home.

It's absolutely perfect. I wanna live here!

I feel like we've discovered the Shire.

AH! JOHN. There's even a handle in the middle of the door!

I *could* actually stay here forever.

The man renting out the cottage is great and warmly welcomes us to this perfect little house.

It has three rooms: a living/bedroom, a bathroom, and a kitchen.

Pretty sure, if it had room for a studio, I'd still be there.

It even says "Shire" on the toilet!

After thoroughly exploring, we have some dinner and watch TV.

Meanwhile, I pencil out a few pages.

I wind up having some pretty strange dreams that night, but the one that I remember the most later is...

Is that a rainbow?

Hmm.

I can't seem to get a picture.

Every time I try to take a picture, it sinks below the horizon.

I wake up fairly early, as my brain is still sorting out what time zone I'm in. I lay and ponder my dream.

The morning is quiet, peaceful. We take our time.

Before we delve into family stuff, John and I drive about without a map just to see where we end up.

uh.

Left?

Right!

! Aughnaclitt

RIGHT!

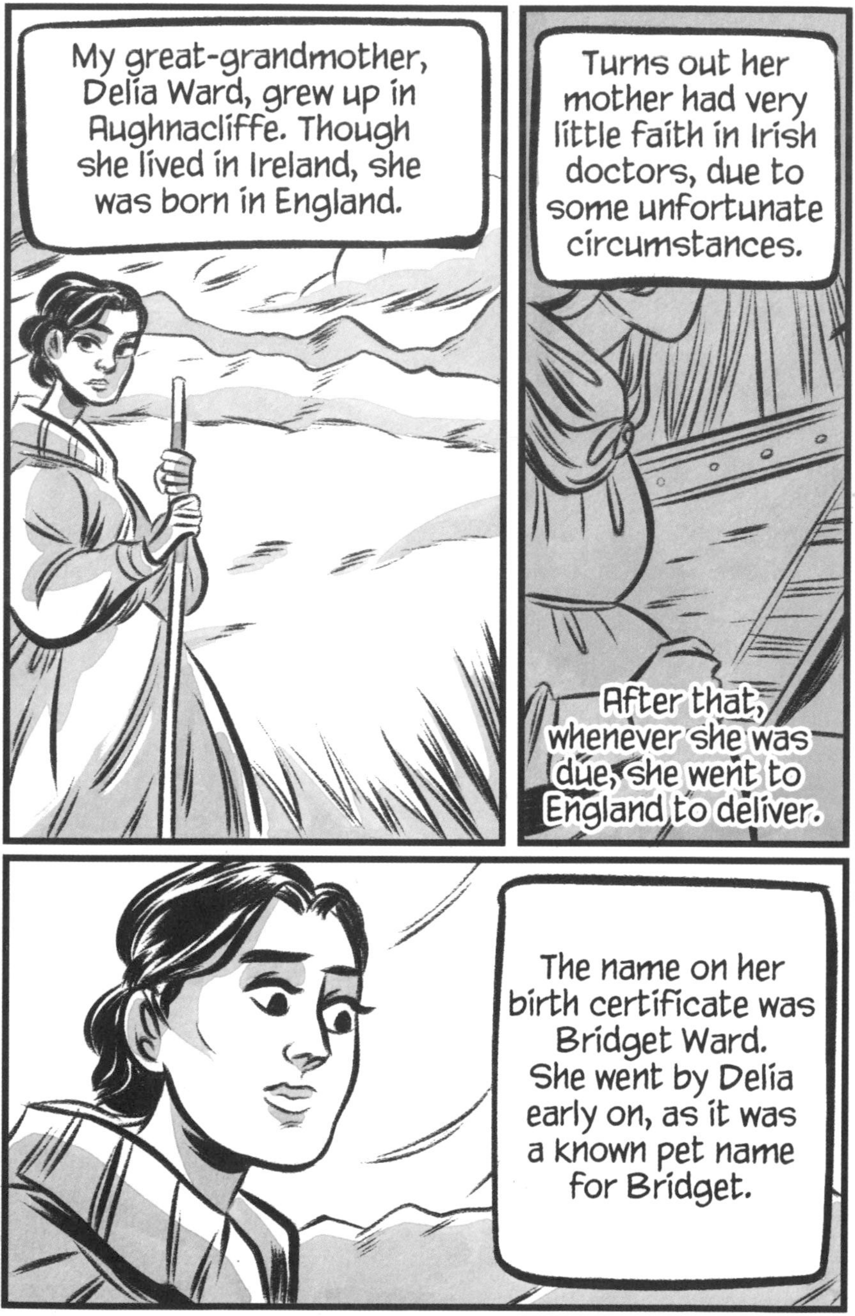
My great-grandmother, Delia Ward, grew up in Aughnacliffe. Though she lived in Ireland, she was born in England.
Turns out her mother had very little faith in Irish doctors, due to some unfortunate circumstances.
After that, whenever she was due, she went to England to deliver.
The name on her birth certificate was Bridget Ward. She went by Delia early on, as it was a known pet name for Bridget.

My dad's cousin was able to get a copy of a book, *A Walk Through Fostra*, by Sean Farrell. In it are some details on the Ward farm that Delia grew up on, as well as info on the surrounding area.

The map in the book, being from the 1800s, is hard to decipher as a current map. Land has been bought and sold many times since then.

The Ward farm passed through many hands. I'm not even certain it's still functioning as a farm at this stage.

We assume that Delia met Edward O'Connor while in America.

Though they were said to be living in Staten Island, they wed in Manhattan in 1909.

It was at that time that she started going by Della. She thought it sounded more American.

She was a tough lady from what I've been told. Of the kids she had, she lost two of them early on.

Compared to that, what are *my* problems? If she could keep moving forward after that...

Sadly, this happened to many women of her time. It certainly makes me think.

...perhaps I can too.

After exploring the small town we head down a random street and come across a small lot with access to a lake.

Maybe my great grandma came here at some stage? Maybe she stood right here, once.

It would have been nice to know her.

Loch Gowna Natur

Siuloidi Imshaoil i Loch Gamh

We walk down the road and find a small hiking trail.

It starts to rain, but the trees seem to give us enough cover from the brunt of it.

Ha! John, look!

It's a rainbow!

I remember my dream and feel compelled...

CLK

Got you.

All right, come on, you dork.

It's getting dark, so we head back, but not without first herding some cows.

We have a few drinks when we get back to the house...
(Club Orange and rum.)

...and listen to some tunes while we cook up some food.

Pasta Bolognese!

We venture outside in the dark after dinner.

Since we're out in the middle of nowhere, there are so many stars.

I'm used to seeing them, but to John it's more of a big deal.

Being in the city most of the time, he doesn't get to see this. And I must say his excitement about it is quite endearing.

Everything at this very moment feels right.

Like this is exactly where I'm meant to be.

For the first time in a long time, I really feel happy.

And the universe, as if in agreement...

With John's help, I make it inside.

And then, of course, drunken discoveries.

John.

JOHN.

It's one of those tap lights!

Uhhh, so this totally isn't peanut butter.

Oh god. It tastes like biscuits.*

*Biscoff biscuit spread looks just like peanut butter! We messed up!!

And unwind.

AHHHH

I become increasingly aware of my hands. As usual, they're *cold.*

They've oddly been the cause of some grief over the last few years.

Don't touch me with your COLD HANDS

A little thing, but it was just another reason I was pushed away—

Here.

Your hands are freezing.

Um.

Oh. Uh.

Oh dear.

He...

I...

I think... I...

Yes.

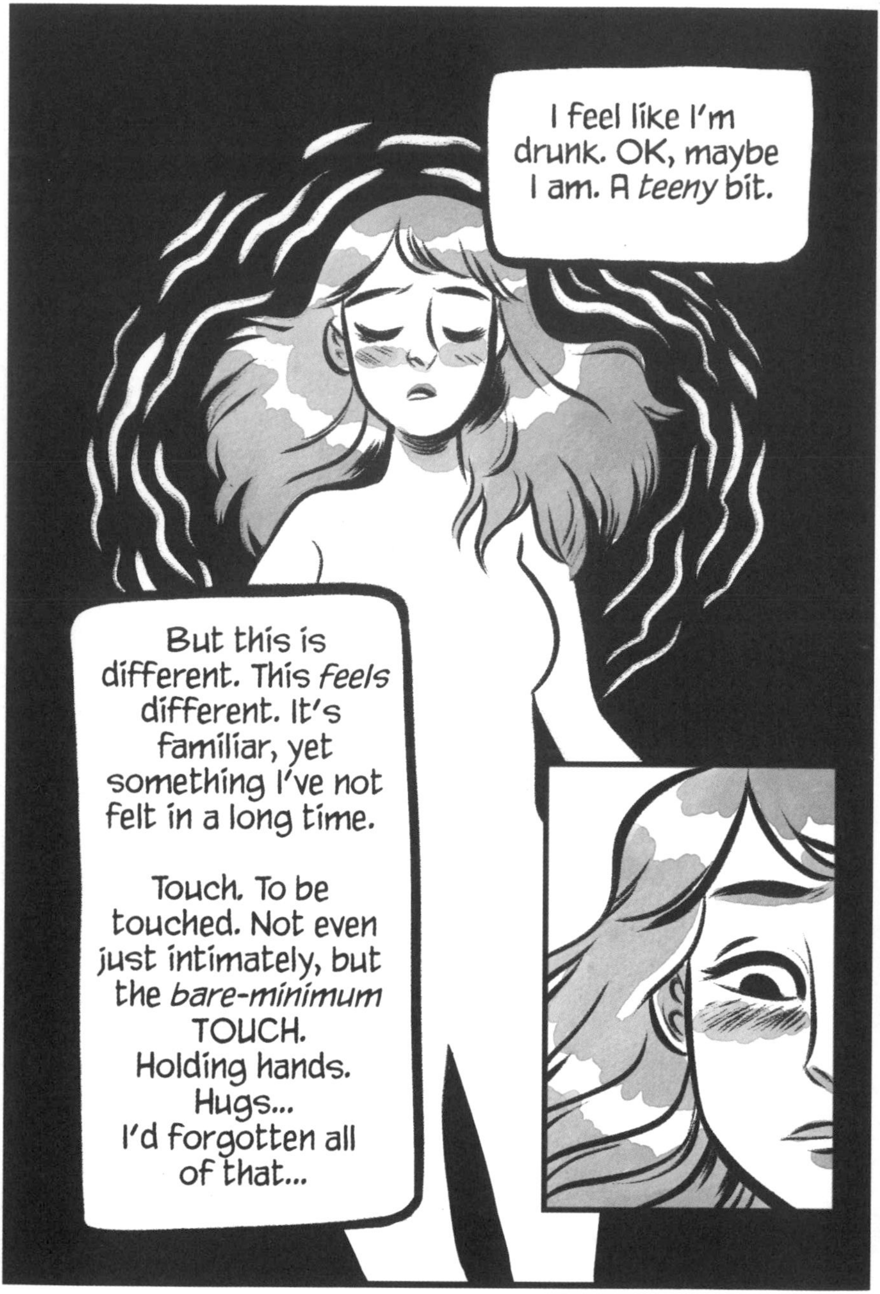
I feel like I'm drunk. OK, maybe I am. A *teeny* bit.
But this is different. This *feels* different. It's familiar, yet something I've not felt in a long time.
Touch. To be touched. Not even just intimately, but the *bare-minimum* TOUCH. Holding hands. Hugs... I'd forgotten all of that...

Years of cold, passionless pecks and forced hugs.

To hug someone and feel their body stiffen, recoil...

To reach out, only to be pushed away...

It's something I'd never wish on anyone.

But now... to suddenly be consumed by this passion, this warmth ...

It's overwhelming, but in the most amazing ways. I feel like I'm being thawed out, like I'm slowly waking up from a dark and dreamless sleep.

I wake up the next morning with my head spinning. For an hour or so I lie there, thinking. It's been a long time since I've been so happy, but at the same time, I'm a little scared, too.

My thoughts keep going back and forth between...

EEEEEEEE

GIRLY FEELINGS!

EEEEEEP

HUMAN EMOTION!

I can't deny my feelings for him...

...they've been there for quite some time.

So do I keep my guard up?

YOINK

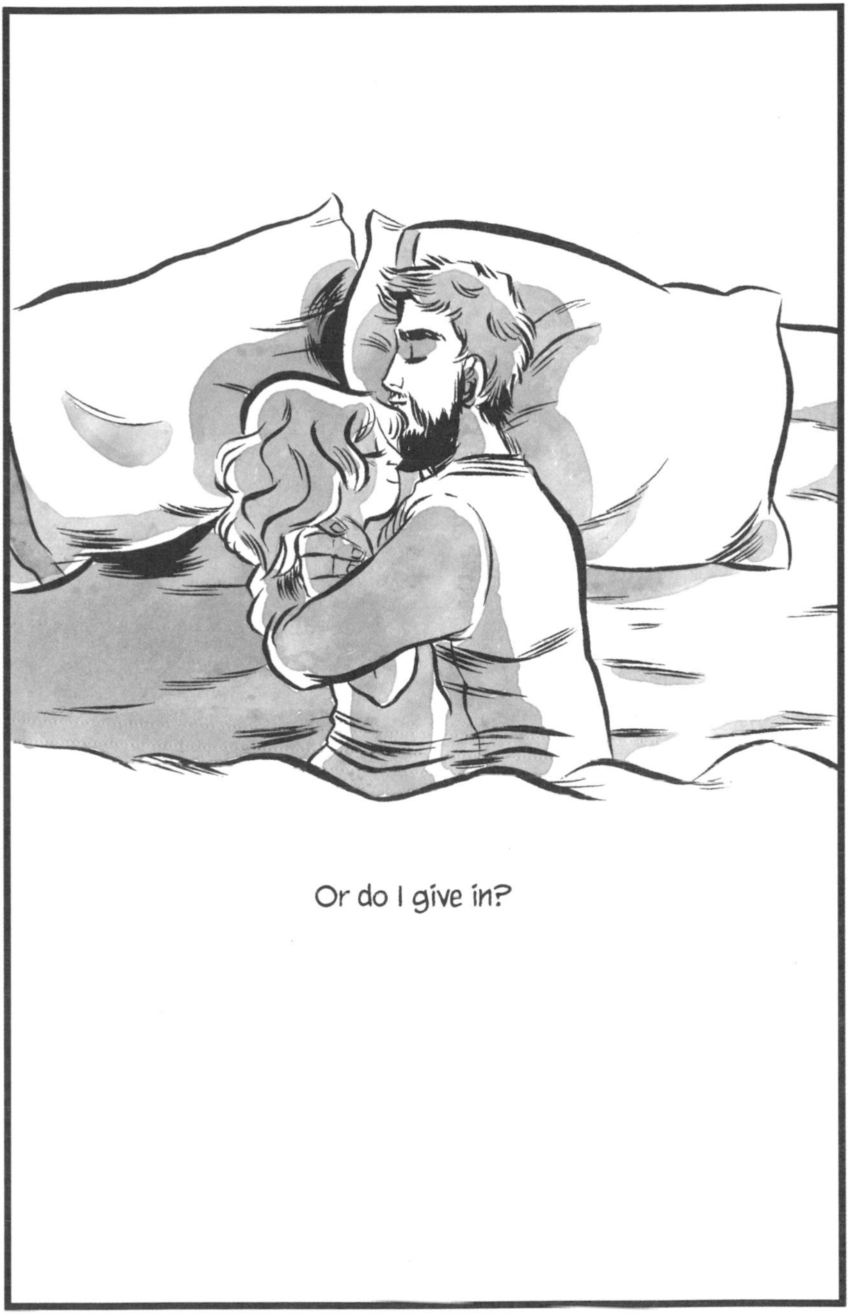
Or do I give in?

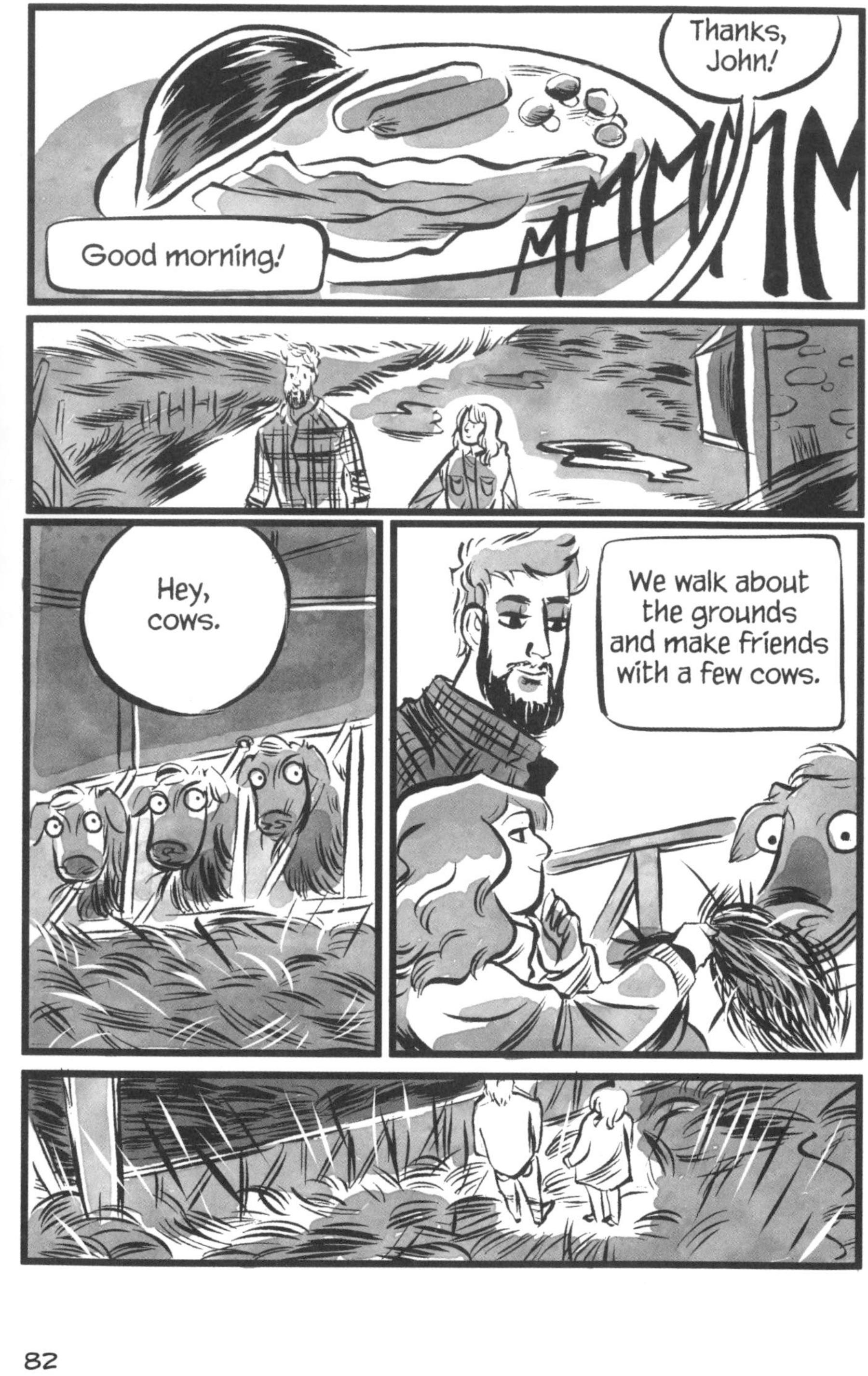
Thanks,
John!
Good morning!
MMMMMM
Hey,
cows.
We walk about the grounds and make friends with a few cows.

The rain chases us inside, but we don't mind.

What's better than a night in playing games and drawing comics?

I finish writing up my notes for the day and sketch out a few pages.

I can't stop writing the word "happy."

The night before we're supposed to leave, the wind rages. One of the doors on the barn in the back keeps banging shut, waking us.

BANG CLANG THUNK

Though, truth be told, I'm already awake.

You OK?

With my gut wrenching unreasonably and my head spinning, I find comfort being wrapped up in strong arms and warm blankets. I don't know what is wrong, but damn it, I don't want to leave.

The morning brings calmer weather.

Tara, the cows are staring at me.

Oh, good. They didn't blow away.

Time to clean and pack up and head north, back to Belfast.

There's a weird feeling I can't place. It dawns on me that my trip is nearly over.

I drive back up north in a cruel amount of pain, and John says his folks suggest going to the ER.

MA

1:15

What do you think we should do?

I think your best bet would be to go to the hospital.

It's not too crowded, but we're told that the wait can be kind of long.

Name?

Like, 6 hours kind-of-long.

So we may be here a while.

Um. Tara.

I'm sorry ...

If you want, you can go to uni while I wait.

I feel really bad at this point, because John was supposed to head in to his university today to get some work done.

But instead, we're here.

Once in the back room, they check my blood pressure, heart rate, and temperature. They ask for a slew of symptoms, and, while I have a pretty good idea of what it is, I'm still not one hundred percent sure. They proceed to check my heart rate for a second and third time.

Your heart seems to be racing. Is this normal?

Um, well, I am a bit anxious

...

but I don't think that's abnormal?

I mean, I'm in a foreign country at a hospital, so yes, I'm a bit nervous.

Nevertheless, they decide to run a few tests anyway.

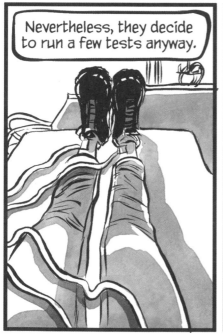

I'm getting more and more anxious by the second...

I did not budget for this...

I make polite chatter with the doctor while I get drained and spot a nervous John watching from the waiting room...

Thank you, awesome doctors! Thank you, NHS!

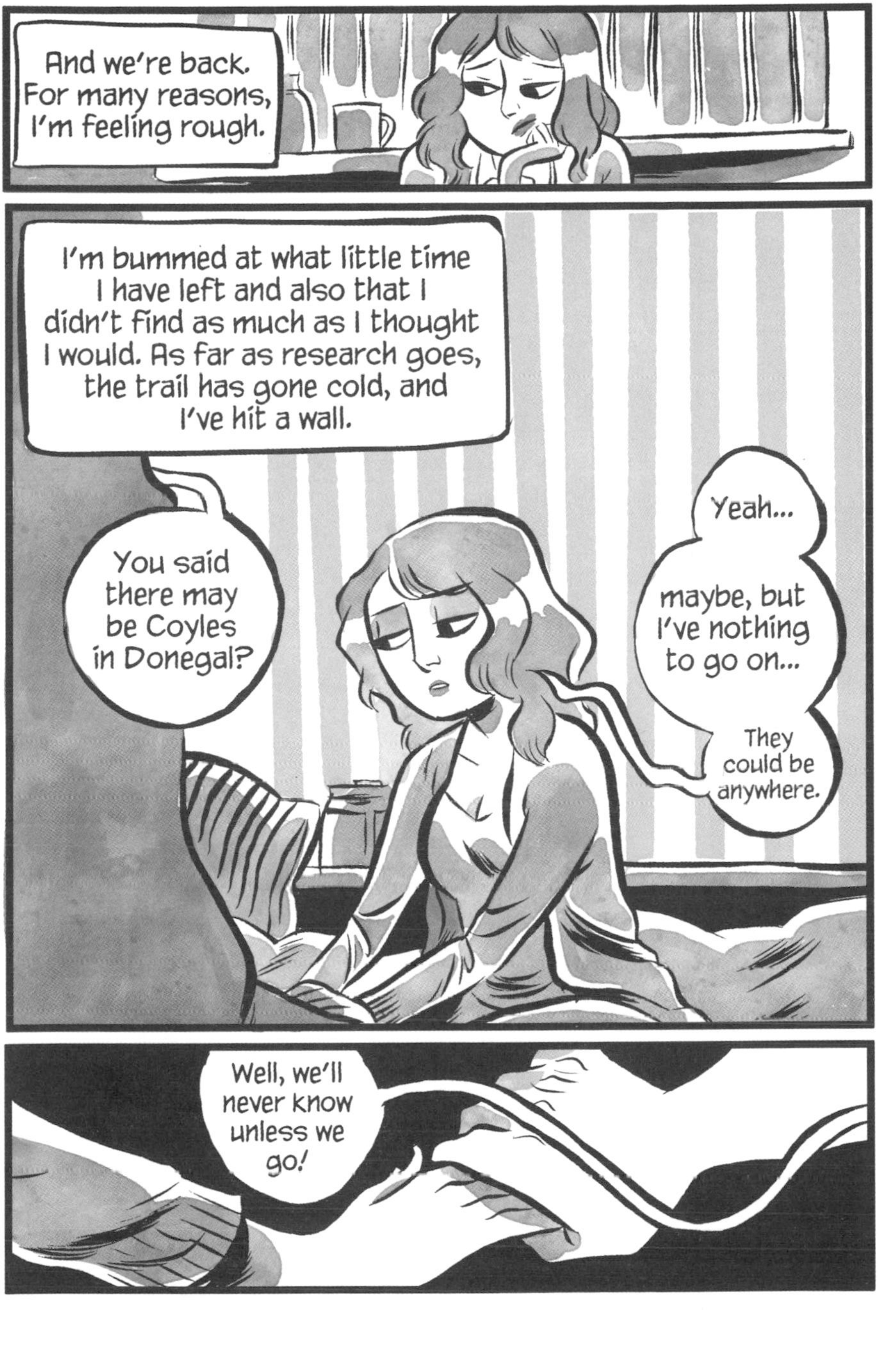

And we're back. For many reasons, I'm feeling rough.
I'm bummed at what little time I have left and also that I didn't find as much as I thought I would. As far as research goes, the trail has gone cold, and I've hit a wall.
You said there may be Coyles in Donegal?
Yeah...
maybe, but I've nothing to go on...
They could be anywhere.
Well, we'll never know unless we go!

We grab a bus from Belfast...

And that's where the offices for Uproar Comics are!

TO DERRY

Oooo

TO DONEGAL

We arrive fairly late in Donegal and we're beat.

We flee to the nearest hotel...

Do you have any vacant rooms?

Pretty please?

Um.

Yes.

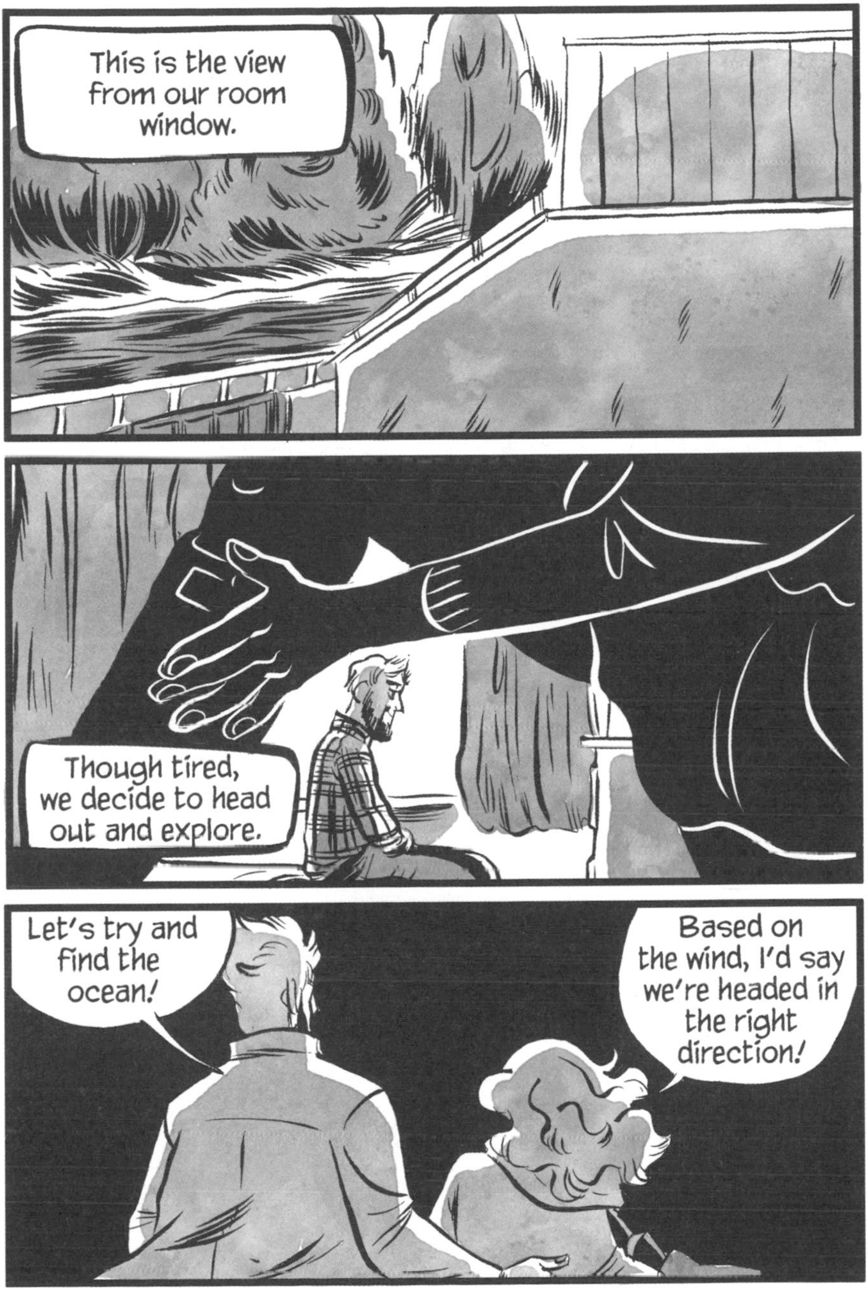

This is the view from our room window.
Though tired, we decide to head out and explore.
Let's try and find the ocean!
Based on the wind, I'd say we're headed in the right direction!

We make it down to the water and walk along the pier. There are railings, docks and boats, and the occasional streetlight to guide our way.

The wind is so fierce against our ears that neither of us can hear the other.

We reach the end of the pier and look out into nothing.

It's like we're at the edge of the world.

Look! A grave-yard!

The Donegal Abbey graveyard was formerly a Franciscan abbey, its ruins now used as a cemetery.

It's eerie, but beautiful, even in the darkness.

Here, I can use my phone as a torch.

Uhhhh...

I think we're stepping on someone.

Awh crap.

I'm really sorry, dude!

We reach the end of the line and head down the hill.

No Coyles, but there were tons of others...

Entire families remain together, even in death. How morbidly touching.

My phone dies, but we hold each other close and move slowly along the narrow path back to the pier in the darkness.

The pier is more than deserted now, and the cars that were there are gone. John amuses me with future plans...

I think I want a power boat.

Yeah?

Drinks?

YEP.

We find a small, cozy pub in the center of town and get out of the wind for a while.

We talk about some deeper things over drinks and have a few laughs as well.

You hungry?

We grab some food, head back to the room, and watch some TV.

Compared to my father's, my mother's side of the family, the Coyles, is much harder to find. The issue here isn't names or dates, but rather, locations...

There are hints to their whereabouts, but they seem to pop up everywhere.

Some in Donegal, some in Ulster, some in Dublin, or even further south still.

COYLE

My great-great-grandfather, John, was born in 1861. He grew up in New York City.

However, his parents, Owen and Annie, were both born in Ireland.

I'm not able to find out where they came from or when (or if) they immigrated.

John married in 1874, at 13, to Margaret, who was 10.

Margaret Templeman was born in Ireland, though her birth town is unknown. Her immigration year is listed as 1871.

They lived in Manhattan with their 9 children...

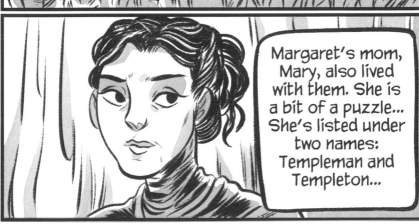

Margaret's mom, Mary, also lived with them. She is a bit of a puzzle... She's listed under two names: Templeman and Templeton...

I'm not able to find much on her, other than that her birth year is listed as 1820.

Margaret was her only child, so it seems she was widowed OR she never married. There is an account of a Mary Templeton on an incoming passenger list, as a vagrant.

So whether that was her and she changed her name, or it was someone else entirely, I can't be sure.

I really wish I could find where they came from...

a town, a county...

...but as of now, that trail has gone cold.

And I've run out of time.

The next day we grab a bus and head further south toward Galway. About halfway down the coast we switch buses and continue on. The views are spectacular.

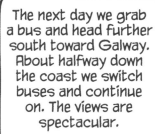

I find it hard to focus on my notes...

While it sucks that we only had the car for a week or so, the plus side to taking the bus is that I actually get to take in the scenery.

With mountains on one side of me...

...and the ocean on the other.

The bus ride is long, and we're both exhausted. I take a short nap, and, before I know it, we're in...

GALWAY!

We grab some food and manage to get a hotel room nearby.

Heh. You were right!

They didn't understand you; they put your name as "McFordon."

HA!

Once fed, we venture out of our room and into town...

Comics comics comics.

Comics comics comics.

We find a bar and talk shop.

Unfortunately, being in the bar setting, we find ourselves assaulted with the typical bar music...

bringing sexy bac

Oh god, no.

This song.

Uh... ick.

Chug your beer, hurry!

We escape into the night and walk around town. We stop at a bridge and look out...

"You should move here," John says.

And I would... in a heartbeat.

Our trip to Galway feels more and more like a bust. It was fun, but as an impromptu trip, we don't have a lot of time for research.

We spend most of Sunday on buses and trains heading back to Belfast. I only have a week left, but I don't even want to think about it. The thought of leaving makes me queasy.

I didn't expect this. I spent the last few years brokenhearted, and now it's like I'm finally starting to *feel* again...

...and it's equally as wonderful as it is painful.

I love it.

The next day we go over to John's uni, where he's doing a residency.

He's been working on some animation projects and storyboards. I meet a few of his mates before he gets started for the day.

UNIVERSITY OF ULSTER

While I'm working on pages, there's a class in session...

Make sure you're working on separate layers!

Maybe I should consider going back to school so I can teach at a higher level...

The next day is a work-from-home day. We spend some hours in John's room as I work on *Roots* and he gets some concepts drawn out. It's cramped, but comfortable.

I've always loved being able to share a space like this. Talk things out, share ideas. It's inspiring.

The next few nights are a bit more social as we head out to see one of John's mates play an open mic.

VOOD

I talk a bit about where I'm from, and my disdain for Bon Jovi quickly makes itself known.

There's a bit of snide laughter, but I think nothing of it...

...until...

It's all the same...

*And that I've now put that fact in writing?! I'm losing all my cred here.

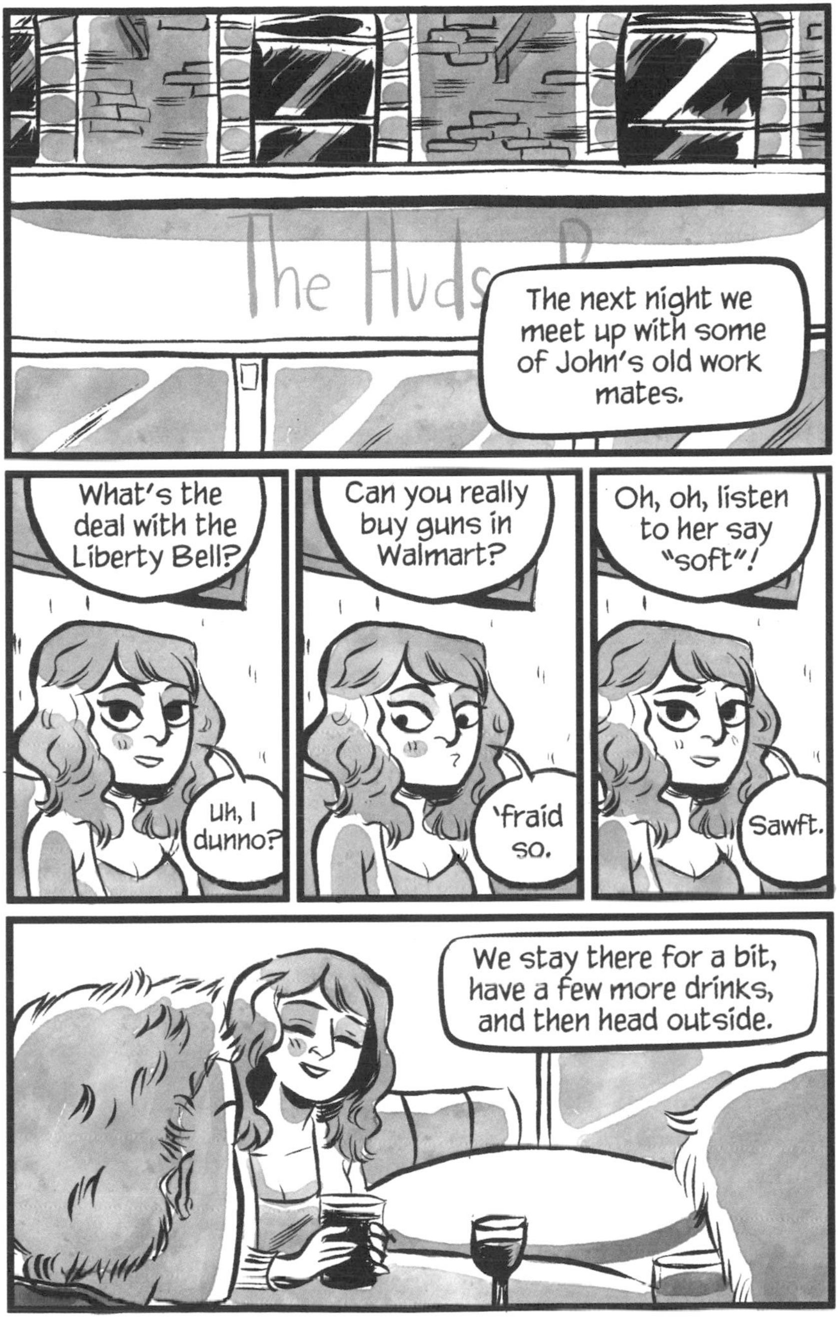
The Huds
The next night we meet up with some of John's old work mates.
What's the deal with the Liberty Bell?
Uh, I dunno?
Can you really buy guns in Walmart?
'fraid so.
Oh, oh, listen to her say "soft"!
Sawft.
We stay there for a bit, have a few more drinks, and then head outside.

Someone asks me...

Is Ireland how you expected it to be?

And I have to stop and think about that one...

Honestly, never having been out of the States before, I wasn't sure what to expect. The country itself is gorgeous, and the people are very friendly—but there wasn't anything that was particularly jarring or unexpected.

A lot of people, when they travel to foreign countries, focus on the differences, but what I most noticed were the similarities. After a few days it just felt like home.

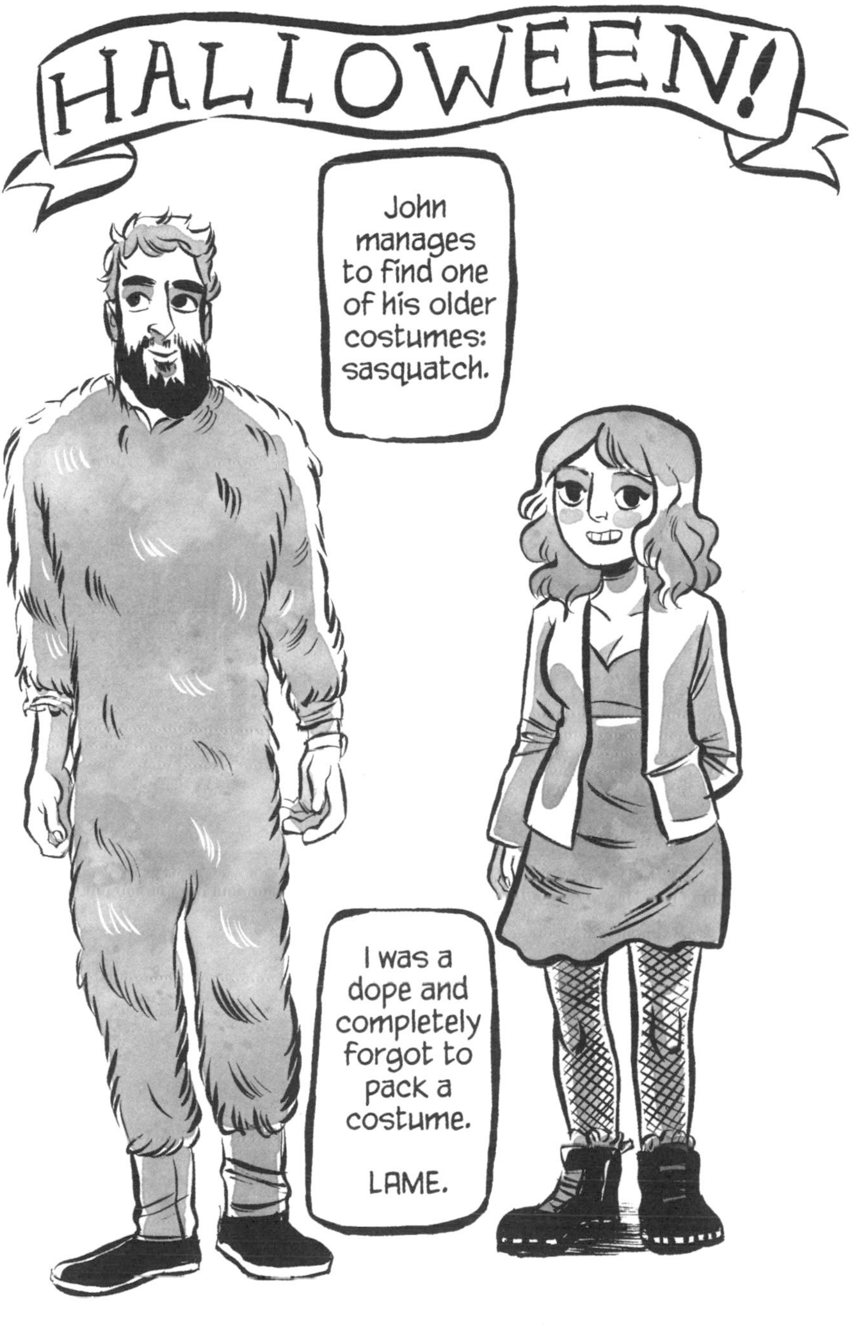
HALLOWEEN!
John manages to find one of his older costumes: sasquatch.
I was a dope and completely forgot to pack a costume.
LAME.

Celebrate Halloween at **CLUB HELL**

We dance like fools to 90s metal.

We have a bet going: how many dudes dressed as ladies?

I say 7.

Nah, at least 10.

Final count: 6 (John wins, *sorta!*)

And with more drinks...

...comes more music and more dancing.

We follow the crowd and pick up a couple pizzas.

While we get some air we witness some...

Hey, hey! You can't buy this anywhere else!

...illegalities.

Despite the hour we manage a taxi...

...and, finally: home.

And now it's Saturday, which means that tomorrow we take a bus down south to Dublin. Two days left.

We spend most of the day around the house, and I reluctantly pack up my things...

So, when do you want to

...

AGGHHH! NO, no, stop making that face!*

*John's Kryptonite

These last few days come with a heavy heart. I've been here nearly a month, but it feels like it's only been days. It's hard to face leaving the place *and* the person that have made me the happiest I've been in years.

We take a walk to the Asda,* and I pick up a few things for John's folks as a thank you.

*local supermarket

John has me navigate our way back to the house.

Go left!

Ha! Yes!

Time to head back to Dublin.

I say my goodbyes to John's folks...

Thanks!!

...get a taxi...

...and hop on the bus. I spend most of the ride down in a complete daze.

We arrive at the airport in what feels like the blink of an eye. Thankfully, I don't fly out for another 18 hours. Though I contemplate how fast that time will go.

I get a message from a friend of mine back in the States: "Don't leave with any regrets and say everything that you need to."

We get off the bus
and head to the hotel
in the rain.

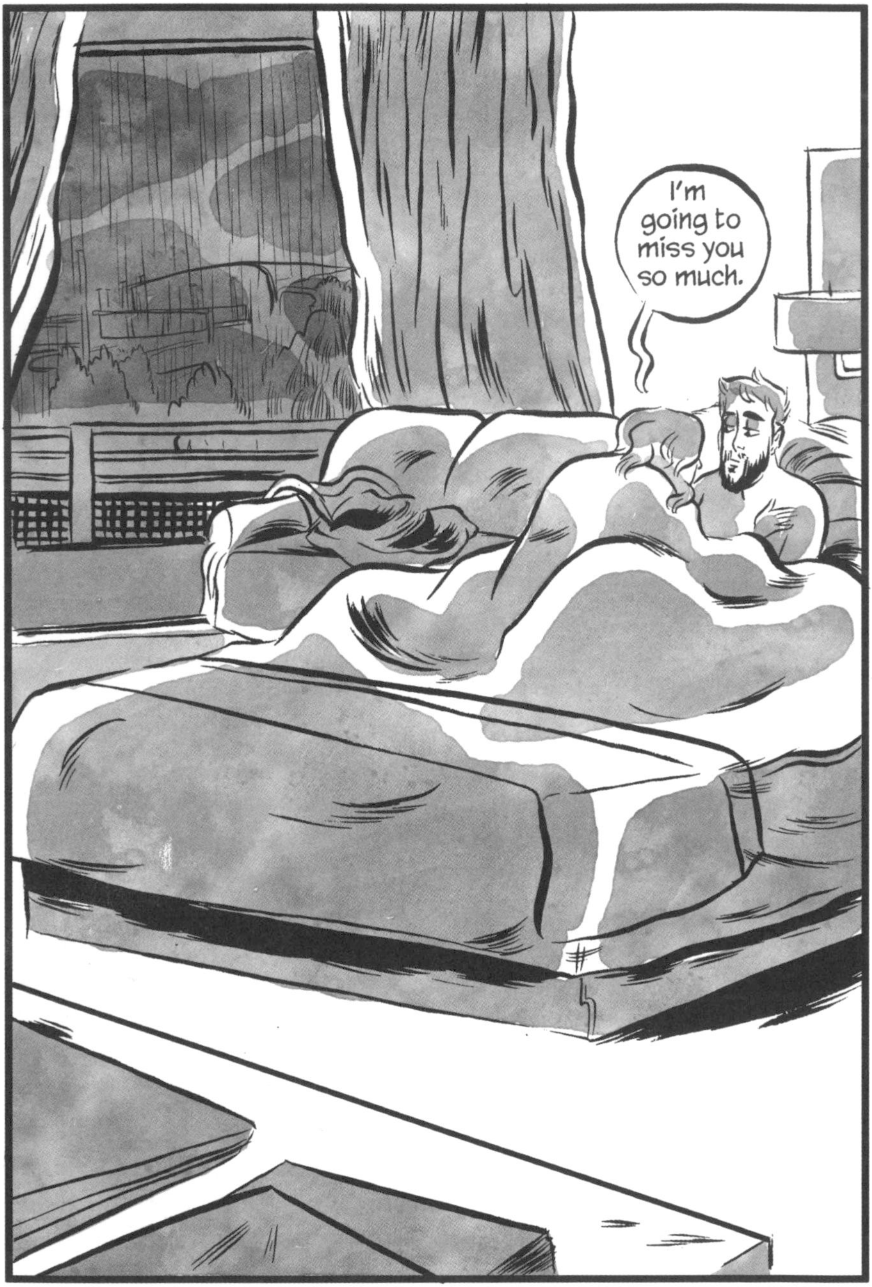
I'm going to miss you so much.

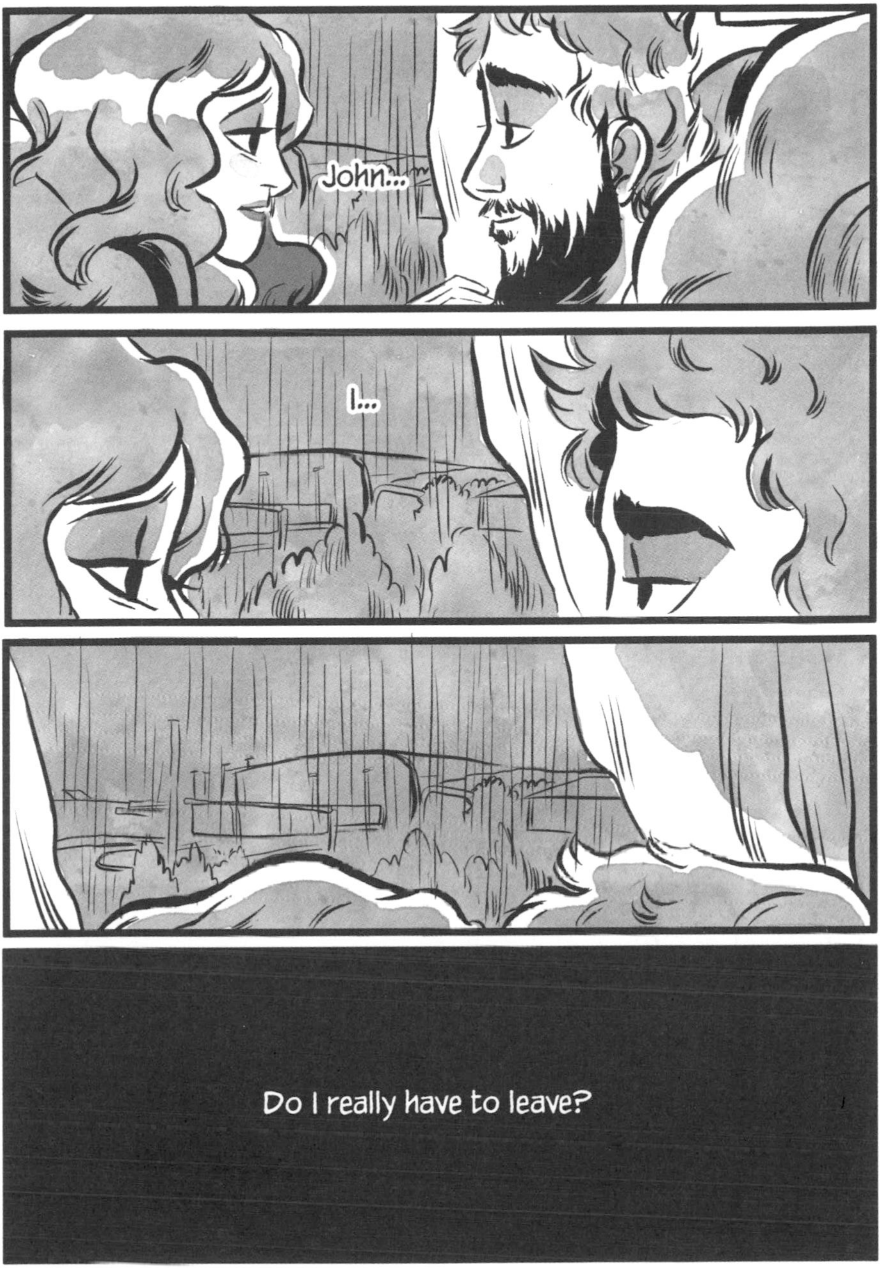
John...
I...
Do I really have to leave?

We put on some movies, hoping to distract ourselves from thinking too much about having to leave.

...Don't we make ya laugh? Aren't we fuckin' funny??

It doesn't *really* work, seeing as I may be the only person to ever get weepy while watching *The Devil's Rejects*.

I don't want to sleep. At this point it's just a waste of the time that I have left...

Do you think you should nap?

NOOOOOOO

Nevertheless, time moves on, and, before we both know it, it's time to head over to the airport.

5:00

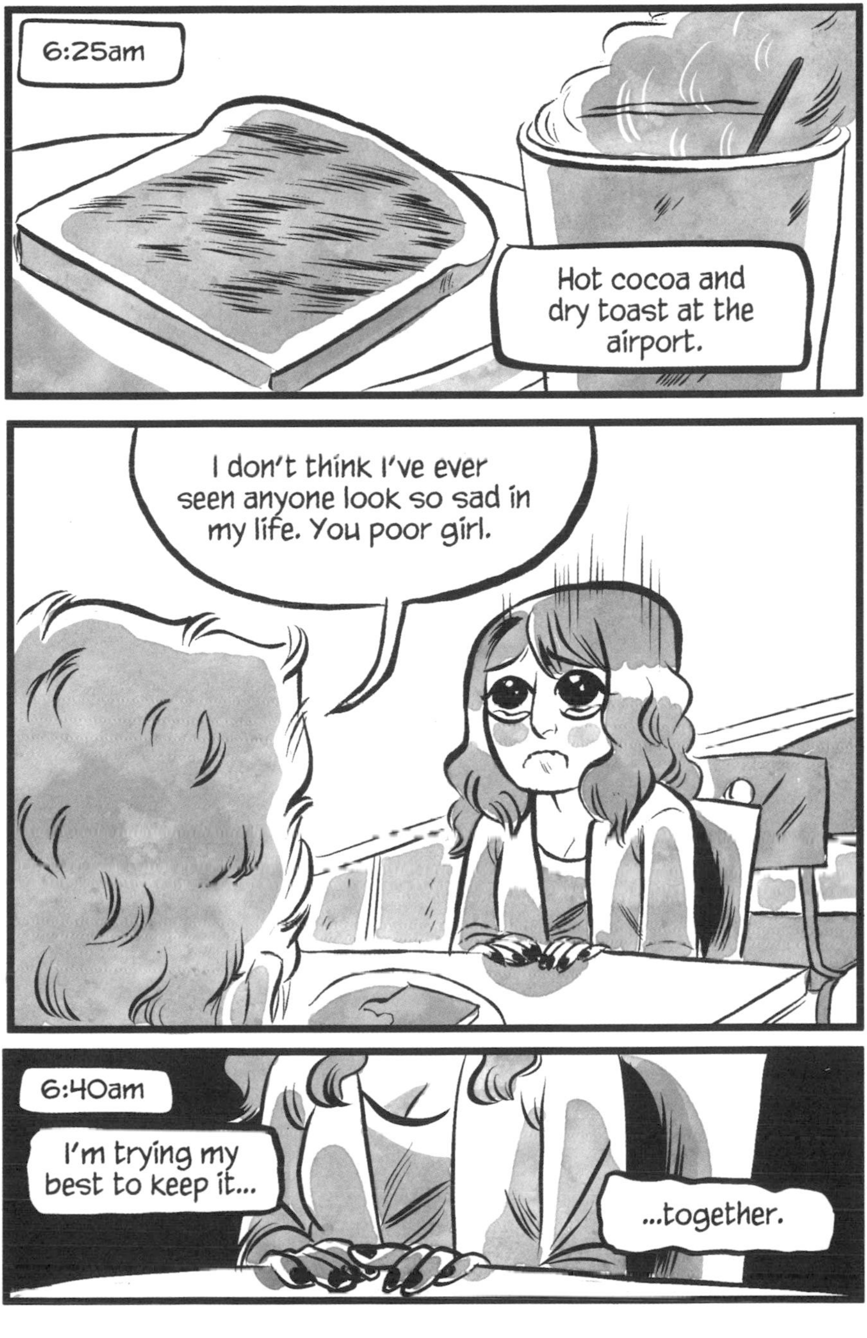
6:25am
Hot cocoa and dry toast at the airport.
I don't think I've ever seen anyone look so sad in my life. You poor girl.
6:40am
I'm trying my best to keep it...
...together.

John walks me as far as he's able to, and we hug for as long as we can. This has been one of the best months of my life. Of all the things that could've happened on this trip...
I wasn't expecting to fall in love.

And I did, *like a ton of bricks.*

Say it, Tara, say it.

If you don't say it, you'll always think back and wish you had.

I love you.

Don't make me let go.

There's no line for security. Afterwards I head to the USPC...

...which feels worlds away.

Just a few minutes ago, he was there. I was there, and now I'm here.

I just make it to the gate before I break down.

The plane ride home is dreadful. I do my best to force myself to sleep the entire way. I'm partially successful. I do manage to sleep through all my meals...

I'm experiencing a lot of inner conflict... Part of me feels like I've failed. I told everyone I was doing this trip to find myself, to find my past...but did I really? Does anyone ever really find themselves?

Or are we all just making excuses to run away? But the part of me that was the most broken is starting to heal...

...and that's more than I could've hoped for.

I'm back. I spend the next few days jet lagged and miserable. Everything here is still the same.

I know I was gone a month, but now that I'm back it feels like no time has passed. It's like jet lag, but to an entirely new level. Like my time in Ireland was just some wonderful dream.

I receive some flack from folks around me, saying I've fallen too fast...

Go ahead and toss someone off a cliff and then proceed to tell them how quickly or slowly they're allowed to fall.

I go over a few drafts for my Kickstarter update... trying to apologize to everyone for failing ...

type type

I thought I had enough to go on, but it was just roadblock after roadblock ...

Delete Delete Delete Delete

It's clear I was, well, *distracted* while I was over there. (No regrets!)

I start to plan out the book, bit by bit, and I start to get anxious. Would the readers be angry? Angry that it didn't go as planned?

This story that was meant to be all about the past... is slowly turning into my future.

Over the next few months, some things change! I get a job teaching comics!

Back to my roots, yo.

And some things don't change! John and I are as close as ever, despite being so far apart. Though, self-doubt creeps in from time to time...

Love you!

This happens most often in the wee hours of the morning.

PSSSTTT

19 is back.

Why would he bother with you? You're so far away, he could probably have his pick of girls in his own country... prettier ones to boot.

There you go again... he'll find someone better, you'll see. He—

DING Ding!

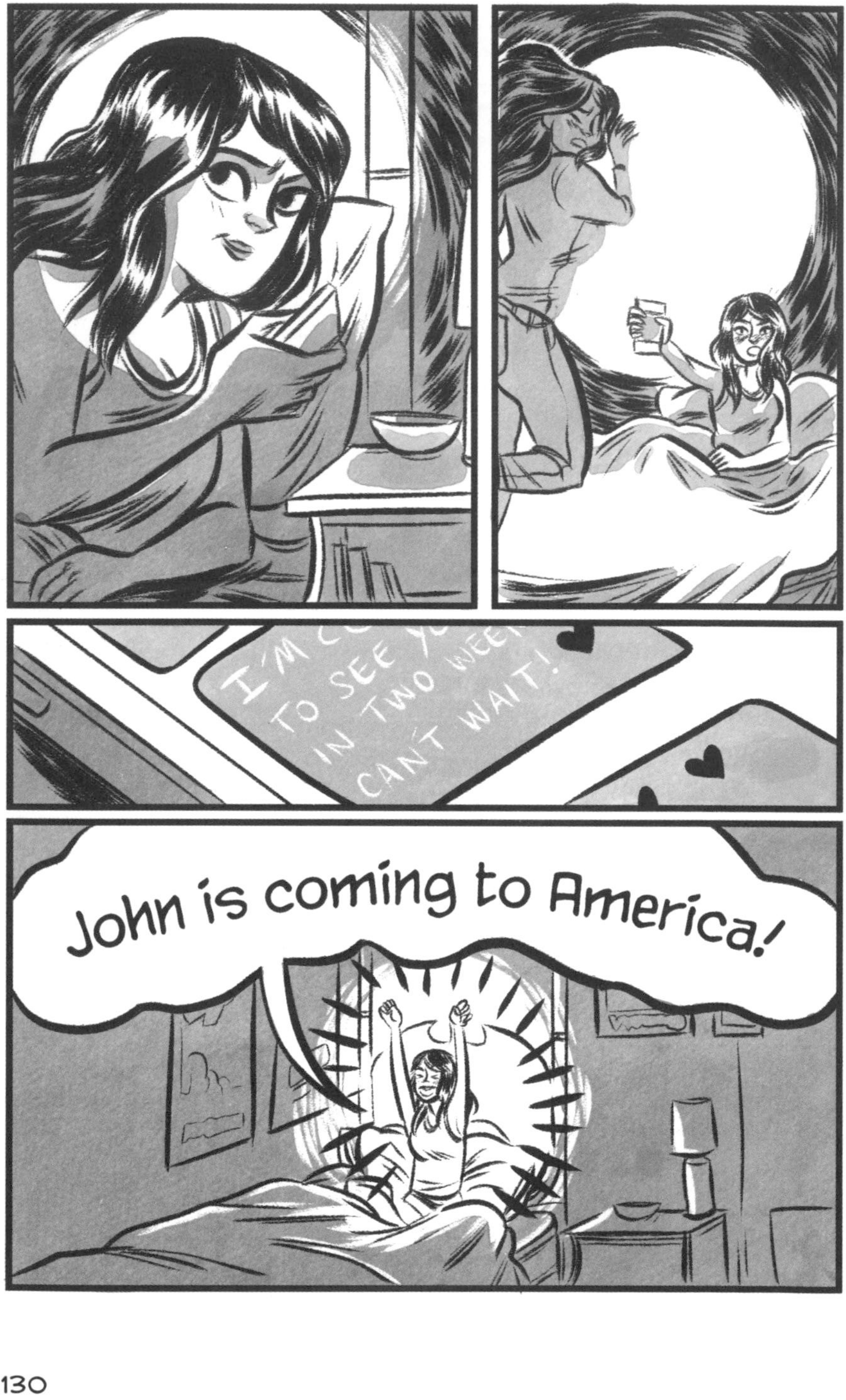
CAN'T WAIT!
John is coming to America!

And before I know it, he's here!

BUP!

SNOW!

Hockey game!

Jersey diner adventures!

Seems as soon as he gets here, he's gone again.

John's first NYC trip!

Swanky NYC hotels!

Thankfully, two months later, I find myself back in Belfast, and John's arms.

Q-Con! John's work is demoing their new game!

OUTSIDER GAM

Much needed alone time!

The zoo!

SLOTH!

Zzzzz

Visit *Comic Book Guys*, the best comic shop in Belfast.

Meet some comic pros!

JORDIE

DECLAN

Talk shop and share the woes of the long-distance relationship.

Aaaand spend the last week sick in bed.

SOON! I promise.

And "SOON" is right! He's surprising me with a visit for my birthday!

His visit coincides with my tabling at SPX! It'll be my first con selling *Roots.**

I pick him up from the airport, and we drive down to Maryland...

...in my old Jeep with no air conditioning.

*self-published, Kickstarter edition

HEY!

We finally make it! I meet a long-time online friend, the talented Claire Connelly! We split a table.

The show is going great! Everyone is so nice. I've done many solo shows, so it's nice to have John cheering me on.

After the show we order a bunch of Chinese food with friends, and John discovers those white take-out boxes are not just TV lies.

They're real!

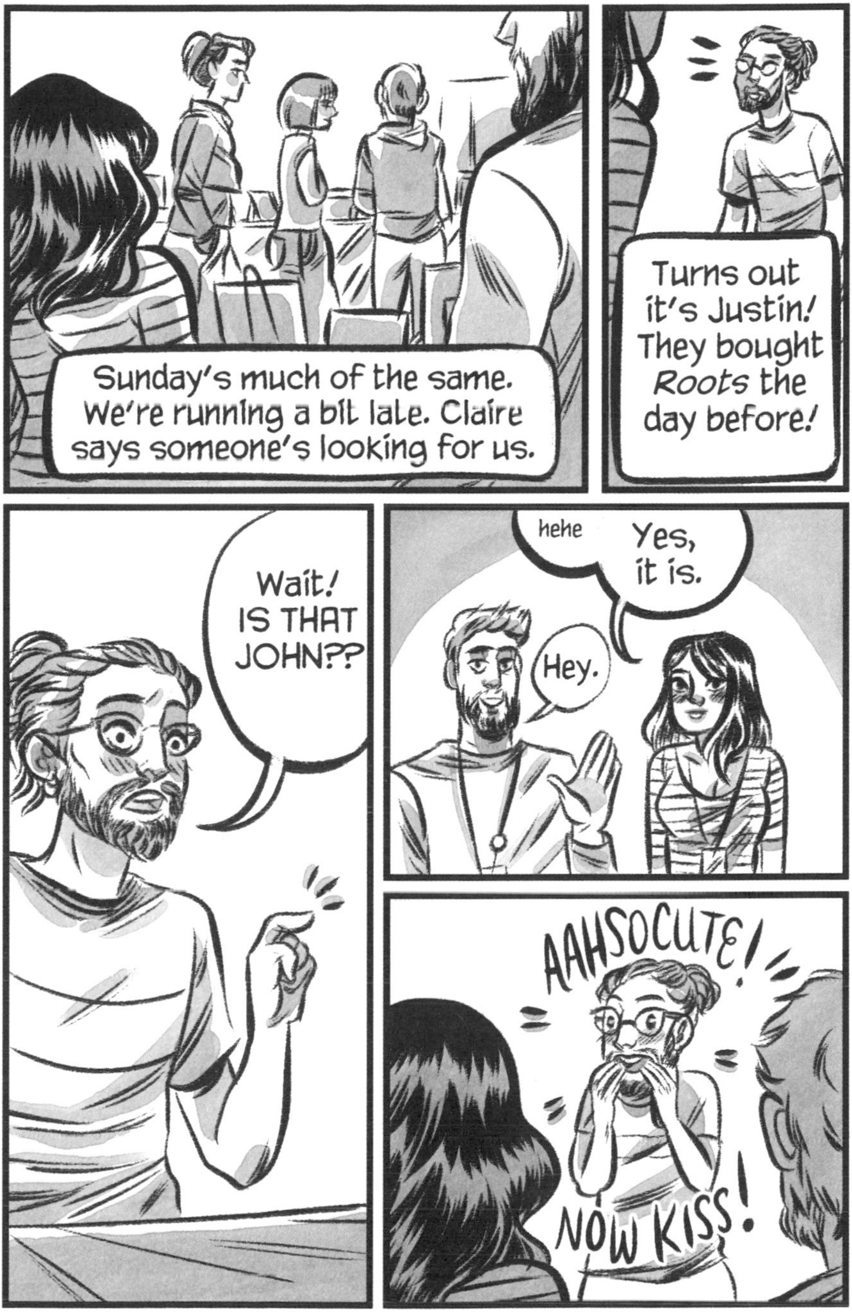

Sunday's much of the same. We're running a bit late. Claire says someone's looking for us.
Turns out it's Justin! They bought *Roots* the day before!
Wait! IS THAT JOHN??
hehe
Yes, it is.
Hey.
AAHSOCUTE!
NOW KISS!

Because it's a short visit, it is over in a blink.

I help him fold clothes and pack his suitcase.

SECUR

And we're back at the airport. Again.

It *really* doesn't get any easier, by the way.

SMOOCH

Two months. We got this.

NOD

The next trip means the most to me. I'm going to be there over Christmas.

Christmas, over the last few years, was a complicated holiday.

It was around this time, years ago, that we lost his mom. And I couldn't do anything...

It was just devastating. I'd never lost a parent, and no matter what I said, or tried, I was shut out. He put up a wall, and it never came down.

Things were far from being perfect before that—hell, they didn't have a chance to begin before they ended.

We rushed in; we knew she didn't have much time...

She was as much a mom to me as my own, but, to him, *I still didn't understand.*

He wouldn't let me understand.

Little by little, every year, Christmas became something I dreaded. It was a cold reminder, not only of losing her...

...but of losing him...

...this person I thought I knew...

...completely.

But finally, after so many years...

I'm once again looking forward to Christmas!

With a week to go 'til Christmas, we venture out to find gifts for everyone.

Take a break to see the new *Star Wars* movie!

I have a bad feeling about this...

We take on wrapping presents together.

On Christmas Eve we Skype with my folks, partaking in traditions...

Ready?

'Twas the night before Christmas when all thro' the house...

It's Christmas morning! We have a quiet morning with tea and cuddles.

I got John the rare Sean Murphy Batman statue!

He got me a new Claddagh ring!

AND a new computer!! (I can finally use my tablet again!)

This blissful morning is all I could ever need or want. Best. Christmas. Ever.

Soon enough, it's New Year's Eve! Despite not having plans, we decide to dress to the nines anyway.

What're you guys all dressed up for?

About twenty minutes to midnight! But wait!

John's roomie decides to join the festivities, so we all say "what the hell" and head out for drinks anyway.

We get there just in time for free Champagne.
(Well, John shared mine.)

We walk down to a bar called Ryan's. It's fairly empty, given the night...

Happy New Year!

It's 2016!

It's 2016.

It's been two years or so since my first trip over. Two years since I started writing *Roots*.

"Roots."

BRUSHA

The word seems to have taken on a new meaning.

It's become less and less about my family roots, and more about where I'll lay down my own.

There's an old saying that I find myself thinking about a lot this morning.

How you spend the first day of the year...

...determines how you'll spend the rest of it.

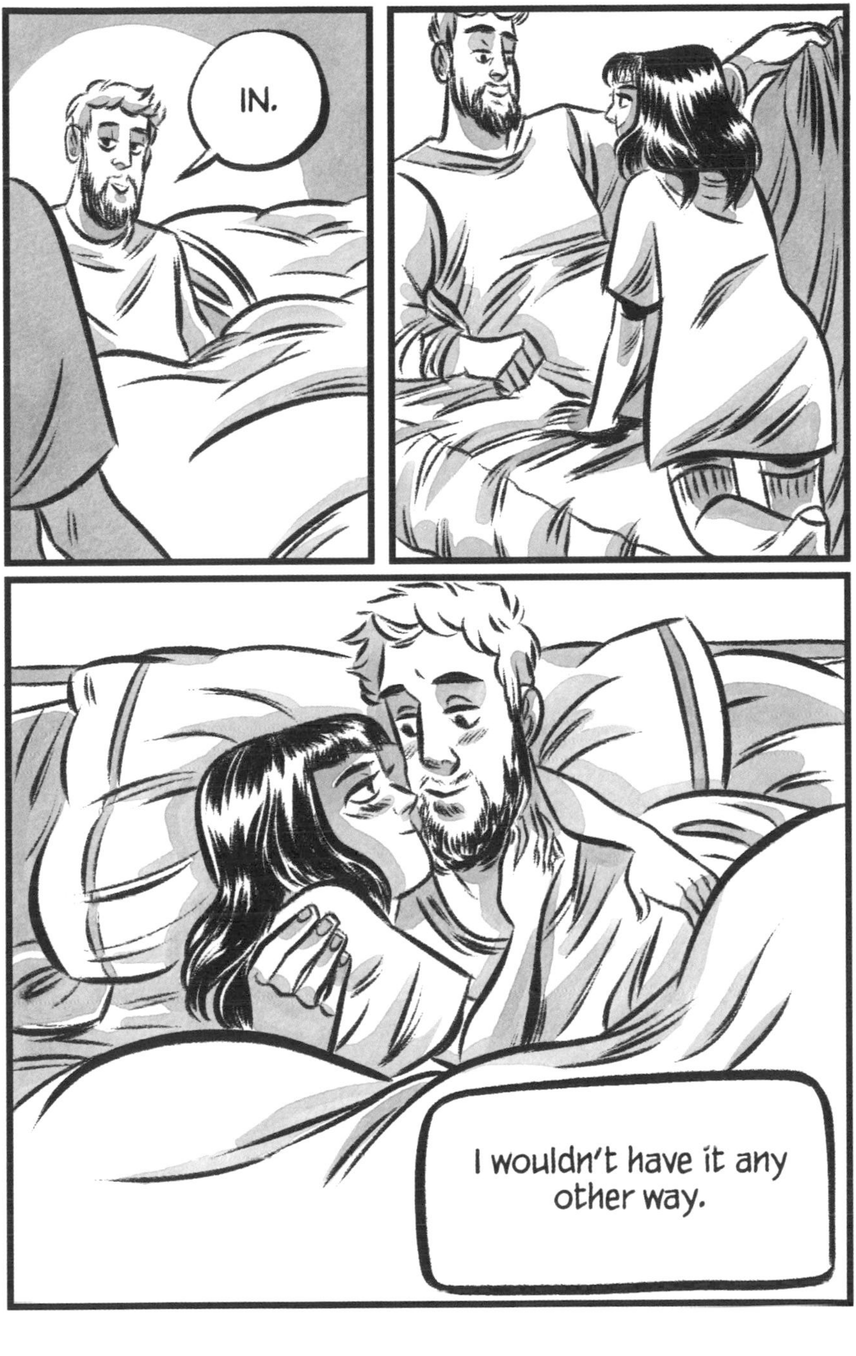
IN.
I wouldn't have it any other way.

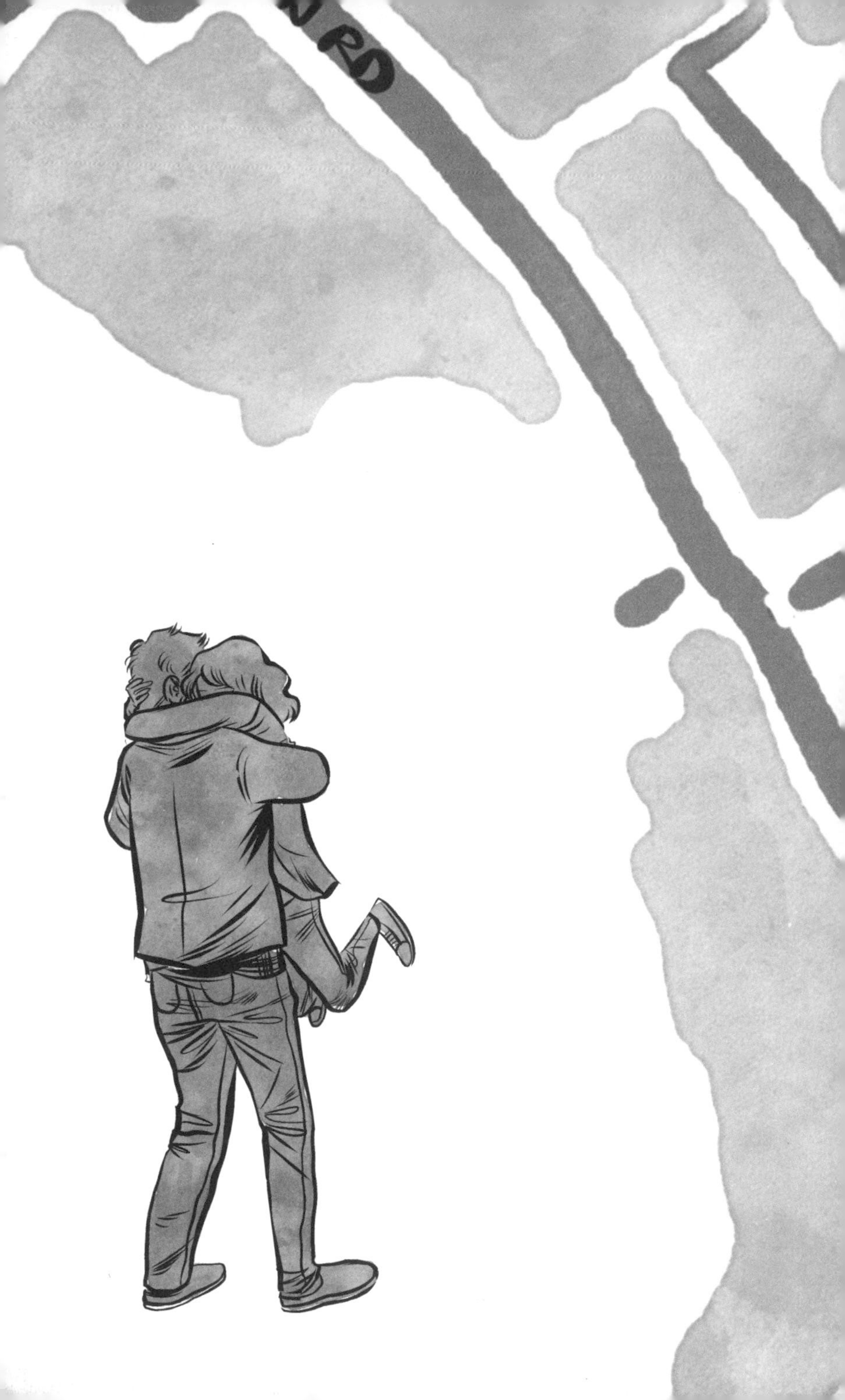
RD